BRITAIN IN OLD PHOTOGRAPHS

KENSINGTON AND CHELSEA

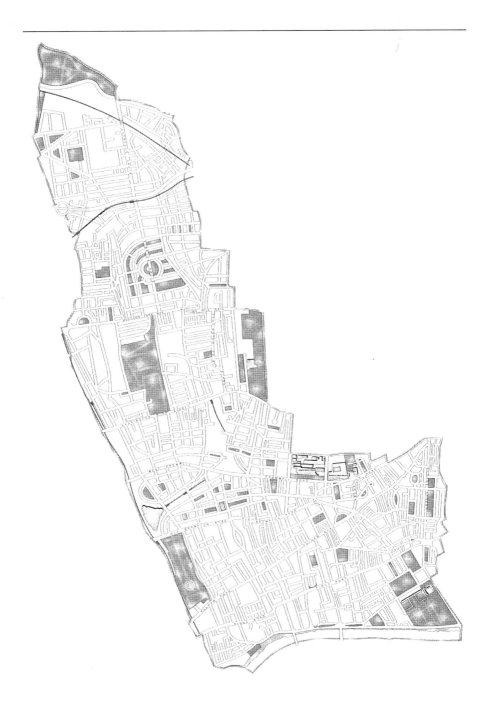

Map of the Royal Borough of Kensington and Chelsea.

BRITAIN IN OLD PHOTOGRAPHS

KENSINGTON AND CHELSEA

BARBARA DENNY and
CAROLYN STARREN

THE ROYAL BOROUGH OF KENSINGTON AND CHELSEA

ALAN SUTTON PUBLISHING LIMITED

Alan Sutton Publishing Limited
Phoenix Mill · Far Thrupp · Stroud
Gloucestershire · GL5 2BU

First published 1995

Copyright © The Royal Borough of Kensington
and Chelsea

British Library Cataloguing in Publication Data.
A catalogue record for this book is available from
the British Library.

ISBN 0-7509-0899-8

Typeset in 9/10 Sabon.
Typesetting and origination by
Alan Sutton Publishing Limited.
Printed in Great Britain by
Hartnolls, Bodmin, Cornwall.

Cover photograph: Kensington's High Street in the 1860s at the junction with Church
Street before Mr John Barker arrived to take one of the shops which were soon to be
swept away by road widening on the south side. The north side, although of course much
changed, is still identifiable today. While the improvement was welcomed by some, others
were critical of the 'gin palace lighting' and adamant that a speed limit of 13 m.p.h. must
be imposed on carriages.

'A singularly heterogeneous kind of spot, very dirty and confused in some places quite
beautiful in others' – this is how Thomas Carlyle described Chelsea in the 1830s, many
years before this photograph was taken in 1870 by James Hedderley, the photographer-
historian. He immortalized the Chelsea scene and particularly its riverside buildings
such as the Adam and Eve inn (seen here third from the left). At much the same time the
artist Daniel Maclise, describing the length of Cheyne Walk from Oakley Street to
Milman Street, with its mixture of shops, houses and taverns, complained of loud-
mouthed bargees, his neighbours' washing lines and crowing cocks.

Contents

Acknowledgements and Bibliography

We would like to thank the following for their assistance in helping us to compile this book: the staff of Kensington and Chelsea Local Studies departments, and John Rogers for his photographic skills that made even the most faded image come alive. We would in particular like to acknowledge the contributions made by Prudential Assurance (p. 14), British Gas plc (p. 26), Kensington Housing Trust (p. 33), Mrs Thackray (p. 35), Eddie Adams (p. 38), Mrs Milne (p. 51) and Harrods (pp. 126–7). Most of all our thanks go to those, past and present, who have given their precious photographs, often anonymously, to both Kensington and Chelsea Local Studies and without whom there would be no book. In writing the captions we referred to the books listed below, most of which sadly are now out of print. However, they are available through the Royal Borough's libraries.

John Bignell, *Chelsea Seen from its Earliest Days*, Hale, 1987

Mary Cathcart Borer, *Two Villages: The Story of Kensington and Chelsea*, W.H. Allen, 1973

Harold Clunn, *The Face of London*, rev. edn, Spring Books, 1970

Barbara Denny, *Notting Hill and Holland Park Past*, Historical Publications, 1993

Sir Geoffrey Evans, *Kensington*, Hamish Hamilton, 1975

Thomas Faulkner, *History and Antiquities of Kensington*, 1820

Thomas Faulkner, *An Historical and Topographical Description of Chelsea*, 1829

William Gaunt, *Kensington and Chelsea*, Batsford, 1975

Florence M. Gladstone, *Notting Hill in Bygone Days*, Fisher Unwin, 1924

Thea Holme, *Chelsea*, Hamilton, 1972

Derek Hudson, *Holland House in Kensington*, Davies, 1967

W.J. Loftie, *Kensington Picturesque and Historical*, 1888

Survey of London, vols 37 (1973), 38, 41, 42 (1986)

Annabel Walker with Peter Jackson, *Kensington and Chelsea*, Murray, 1987

Introduction

The Royal Borough of Kensington and Chelsea, although a union born out of municipal convenience, is so much more than that. It is Brompton and Notting Hill, the Boltons and Bayswater, Holland Park, Earls Court, Campden Hill, World's End and the North Pole, St Quintin Park and Hans Town, the Vale and all the other neighbourhoods which have grown out of either administrative necessity, fashion or snobbery. Yet all these have come from the same beginnings, settlements by the river, or on high ground deemed safe in Anglo-Saxon times, giving rise to the names of Cealchythe or Celchyth – Chesil – a gravel bank, Chenesiton and Knotting Hill, after their tribal overlords or their geographic nature, villages that expanded into 'towns' and merged into each other yet retained something of their early identity. Even today, with no documented or visible boundaries, they have kept their own character and are encouraged by the desire of their residents to remain so.

If the 'birth' of an area can be dated at all, it might be by the establishment of its first place of worship, around which the rest of it grew. For Kensington, then, it must be 1260, when the abbot of the Benedictine Abbey of St Mary Abingdon established a church there, following the bequest of land to his predecessors in Norman times by Aubrey de Vere. In Chelsea, the 'Old Church' dedicated to All Saints also dated from the thirteenth century. Both original churches have, of course, been rebuilt several times.

Change is inevitable in a living community, but the traveller who entered the district in those days may well have journeyed by the same routes that have become our main roads. The Romans dictated the first line from east to west, but even they had to accept the dictates of geography, the streams and the hills, so that their highways have become ours, such as Bayswater Road and Holland Park Avenue, with Kensington High Street as a diversion. Fulham and Kings Roads grew from the need of travellers wishing to reach a destination such as the Bishop's Palace (or manor house) at Fulham or the royal palaces at Richmond and Hampton Court. From south to north the ferries and fords, then the few bridges over the Thames, dictated the lines of the roads that still cross the river.

Archaeological remains, historic buildings and artists' works are the only visual relics of the development of the area, supported by documentary evidence. It was only in the mid-nineteenth century that the photograph became the magic window through which the scenes of the past could be preserved like a fly in amber. In fact the past is never easily wiped away; like a smear on glass it may return even after the cloth has apparently wiped it clean. The fields go but the trees live on in back gardens long after whose who planted them are dead and forgotten, a road still follows the same line because some medieval carter chose that way to ease the toil of his horse.

As little as two centuries ago, the mass of bricks and mortar which fills the 3,014 acres of the Royal Borough today, with its contrasts and contradictions of commerce and culture, elegance and depressing mediocrity, was a collection of rural communities set up round the houses of the rich, aristocratic or merchant, already moving out from a noisy and polluted crowded city centre. First came the Tudors, Thomas More, then King Henry VIII himself, to a modest riverside palace nearby in Chelsea, and the Earl of Shrewsbury and Lord Burleigh in Elizabethan times, before royal favourite Walter

Cope built his own 'castle' on Campden Hill which later became Holland House, the home of the debonair turncoat Henry Rich, Earl of Holland, who lost his head in the Civil War in 1649.

By then, the City merchant and moneylender, Baptist Hicks, later Lord Campden, had also built his stately home on Campden Hill, and by the end of the seventeenth century King William of Orange and Queen Mary set the royal seal on the area by choosing another nearby country house to be the new royal palace at Kensington.

Where the great and the good lead, the rest follow, and in the next hundred years the 'Old Court Suburb' and riverside Chelsea attracted their satellites and their servants. Although by the turn of the eighteenth century the court had left Kensington, it was still a royal residence and it was here that the young Princess Victoria lived for much of her childhood, the home she never ceased to regard with affection and on which she eventually bestowed the title of 'Royal'.

Then the railways came and with them streets lined with houses. Orchards were grubbed up, trees felled and pastures became building sites or brickfields.

When all has gone and the modern road is twice as wide (as in the case of Kensington High Street and Notting Hill Gate) it is difficult to believe that the very ground on which one is standing is the same as that where horses' hooves clattered over cobbles, carts rumbled and cattle were driven on the hoof to Smithfield Market.

Likewise, the heartland of Chelsea having moved from the riverside around the Old Church to the Kings Road, it is practically impossible – even with the aid of the art works of James Whistler and the Greaves brothers – to imagine the wharves, alleys and pubs which clustered beside the water before being swept away by the construction of the embankment. 'Museumland', the proud memorial to Victoria's beloved Albert, survives almost intact, and much of Fulham Road is still strangely nineteenth-century.

In the north where the pigkeepers and scavengers, turned out from a smartening central London, had settled in Notting Dale, there came poverty and squalor as well as industry, gas works and factories, embarrassing those with plans to build mansions for the well-off on the rise of Ladbroke Hill and whose dreams have taken over a century to reach fruition.

But what really matters is people, and it is they who give life to the area, as the shades of their forebears give animation to the photographs of the past. A road sweeper stands for ever with his broom, sweeping the gutter in a high street which horse traffic could make impassable. A schoolgirl, with her violin in a case, crosses the street; a baker's boy pulls his handcart near a barrel organ long silenced; a little dog greets a Victorian lamp-post; a City gentleman goes smartly into the new station to catch a train to business.

Moments of ceremony and sorrow, the extraordinary and the mundane, are caught in the stance and expression of these people, often quite unaware that an unseen eye has focused upon them and an instant of their lives. It is they, as much as the setting in which they are playing a part, which can give this book the magic which it seeks to evoke.

Barbara Denny
April 1995

THE ROYAL BOROUGH

The parish of Kensington, which was to become 'Royal' at Queen Victoria's request, puts out the flags to celebrate her Golden Jubilee in June 1887. Fifty years earlier, at Kensington Palace, she had received the news that she was Queen, and she never lost her affection for the old palace which had been her childhood home. The buildings on the right of this photograph, including the Goat public house, are still recognizable today opposite the first gate into Kensington Gardens and the entrance to Palace Avenue. This section records the early years of the Royal Borough, highlighting the events and personalities which maintained its regal associations.

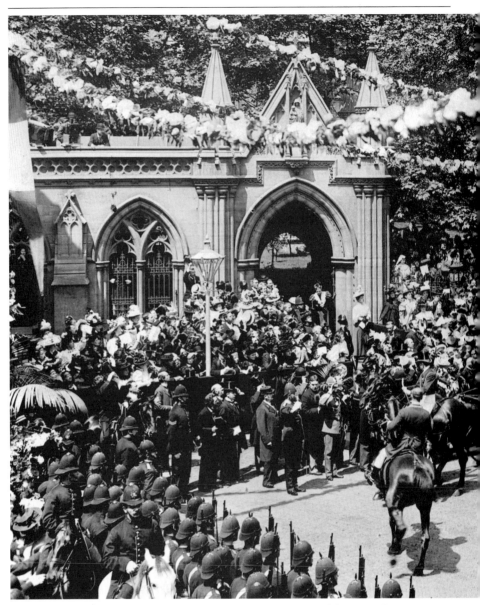

Queen Victoria maintained her love of Kensington into old age and on 28 June 1897, during the celebrations for her Diamond Jubilee, when she was seventy-eight, she paid a state visit to the place where she was born on 24 May 1819. Her carriage is seen here outside the cloistered entrance to St Mary Abbots Church on the corner of Kensington Church Street and the High Street, where the dignitaries waiting to greet her included her daughter Princess Louise and her husband the Marquess of Lorne, Lord and Lady Ilchester, West London MPs and the vicar, the Revd Canon Somerset Pennefather. Mr T. Wheeler, Chairman of the Vestry, presented an address

which a contemporary magazine described as 'slightly more original than usually is the case – to which the Queen gave a most gracious reply'. After receiving a bouquet from Princess Louise and one from Miss Beatrice Leete, daughter of Mr W. Chambers Leete, the Vestry Clerk, the Queen drove off to the chimes of the church bells and the music of military bands. The Royal carriage proceeded at a walking pace so that over 7,000 children from local orphanages, who had been allowed to watch the procession, could get a good view.

On 19 October 1904 Princess Louise unveiled the marble column erected by the people of Kensington at the junction of Kensington High Street and Church Street as a memorial to Queen Victoria. She is seen here being greeted outside St Mary Abbots Church by the Mayor, Cllr J.P. Williams, and aldermen and councillors of what had now become the Royal Borough of Kensington.

King Edward VII and Queen Alexandra driving through Holland Park Avenue on 26 May 1908 on their way to visit the Franco-British Exhibition at the White City, where they witnessed a pageant by Olympic athletes.

Queen Mary visiting Kensington on 22 April 1911 shortly before the Coronation. On her left is the Prince of Wales (later King Edward VIII) and facing them, the Earl of Shaftesbury and Prince Albert, Duke of York, who was later to become King George VI.

On 9 May 1937 Princess Louise planted a tree in the churchyard of St Mary Abbots to commemorate the coronation of her great nephew, King George VI. On her right is the vicar of Kensington, Prebendary Arthur E. Smith.

This postcard, dated 10 March 1905, shows the memorial to Queen Victoria, (designed by H.L. Florence) in more leisurely days, when policemen could stop for a chat without being distracted by traffic and small boys could lean on its base. The archway beyond remains today to the left of the church.

The widening of the High Street in 1934 necessitated the removal of the column from its original site to the northern end of Warwick Gardens. The space was originally intended to be the centre of a garden square until plans changed to give access to Pembroke Road.

King George V and Queen Mary visited Kensington as part of their Silver Jubilee celebrations on 8 June 1935 and are seen here arriving at Kensington Town Hall. Note the cavalcade of royal cars with their high roofs to accommodate the ornate millinery of royal ladies, the elaborate decorations and the fashions of the crowd (almost everyone is wearing a hat).

The east front of Kensington Palace as it appeared in 1898. On the right is the statue of Queen Victoria created by her daughter, Princess Louise, erected in 1893. The room on the lower floor, hidden by trees, was where the Queen was born in 1819; above it are the State Apartments.

View of Kensington Palace taken from the south-west across Palace Green, 1900. Behind the portico on the left is the Clock Court, one of the earliest parts of the palace, dating from the time of the alterations by Sir Christopher Wren and over the centuries the home of various members of the Royal Family up to the present day, including the Princess of Wales, Princess Margaret and the Kents.

In 1895, at the express wish of Queen Victoria, this room in Kensington Palace where she was born, and which had been kept closed for years, was restored to its original appearance and opened to visits by special friends. Its modest, if not austere and rather dreary appearance, contrasts dramatically with the splendour of the Presence Chamber (below), as it appeared a few years later in 1898.

The talent of Princess Louise as a sculptress is evident from this 1900 photograph of her most permanent memorial, the statue of her mother, Queen Victoria, which stands to the north-east of Kensington Palace on the Broad Walk. The sixth child of Victoria and Albert, the Princess was described by the Queen as a 'clever dear girl'. In 1873 she married the Marquess of Lorne (later Duke of Argyll) but the union was not without difficulties and she spent time abroad when her husband was Governor General of Canada. The Princess lived at Kensington Palace from 1873 to her death in 1939 at the age of ninety-one. She worked on her sculpture in a studio in the walled garden of her apartments in the south-west corner.

This photograph shows the statue in 1905 (note the park keeper in pill box hat and brass buttoned coat). Princess Louise became a patroness of many charitable and social concerns in Kensington, especially the Children's Hospital in St Quintin Avenue, North Kensington, which bore her name, the Memorial Playing Fields and the 13th London Regiment of which she was Honorary Colonel. On 31 July 1928 she was made a Freeman of the Borough.

The famous statue of J.M. Barrie's 'Peter Pan' by Sir George Frampton had just been erected in Kensington Gardens when the postcard above was taken in 1912. The monument was set up in secret during the hours of darkness, on 30 April 1912, as if brought there by the fairies that clamber around its base, their heads finely polished by the hands of generations of children. The figure of Peter is said to be based on the six-year-old Michael Llewellyn Davis, one of the brothers who inspired Barrie to write his immortal story and whose guardian Barrie became after their parents' death. The lower picture, taken some eight years later in 1920, shows fashions of the time on summer strollers by the Long Water (the Serpentine).

Children with their nursemaid, shading from the summer heat in the shelter by the Palace Green entrance to Kensington Gardens in 1890, are among the thousands who have similarly sought respite there from sun or rain for over a century. Little has changed but the fashions in clothing and perambulators.

The Alcove, as seen in the 1890s, designed by Christopher Wren for Queen Anne, originally stood in Dial Walk facing Kensington Palace but now stands on the Bayswater boundary of Kensington Gardens. A romantic story is told that in May 1809 a notice appeared on its wall from a love-lorn gentleman begging a young lady he had parted from after a quarrel to contact him urgently.

St Govor's Well stood about 250 yards from the south end of the Broad Walk where these little boys are playing in 1890, but is now covered over. Its waters were supposed to possess medicinal qualities and it is quite likely that its source was connected to the spa which flourished near the gravel pits to the north in the early eighteenth century, where the 'purging waters' were likened to Epsom salts. The well became famous in the 1870s when a Mrs Lacy was given the right to sell water from it for a penny a glass. In 1875 an official enquiry decided the water was unwholesome, but it remained as a drinking fountain – which these boys are enjoying. St Govor was a Welsh saint and the naming of the well is thought to have been the idea of the first commissioner of works in 1855, Sir Benjamin Hall, later Lord Llanover of Lanore, in Monmouthshire, where St Govor founded a church.

The tea rooms in Kensington Gardens in Edwardian times when it was fashionable to be seen taking tea under the elms with service by smartly uniformed waiters and waitresses. A lady's day might well begin with coffee at Fortnums, shopping in Bond Street or Knightsbridge, lunch at the Ritz and tea in Kensington Gardens before a late afternoon visit to Hurlingham or Ranelagh to watch husband or fiancé playing polo. The tea rooms, with outdoor tables, were near the Albert Gate, not far from the Flower Walk and the bandstand where military music was played every summer afternoon and evening by Guards' bands. Leigh Hunt made an impressive list of those who might be seen strolling in the Gardens in 1791. Joseph Addison wrote in *The Spectator* of his admiration of Henry Wise's gardening expertise in 'turning the unsightly hollow of a gravel pit into so beautiful an area', but Sheridan, with classic wit, realized that not all sophisticated ladies feel at home amidst rural delights and has his Woman of Fashion complaining about the trees:

> . . . the spread of their leaves such a shelter affords
> To those noisy impertinent creatures called birds,
> Whose ridiculous chirruping ruins the scene,
> Brings the country before me and gives me the spleen.

The Round Pond, known officially as 'The Basin', edged here with serious Edwardian model yachtsmen, was one of the features created by two famous royal gardeners, Henry Wise for Queen Anne and his successor, Charles Bridgeman, Royal Gardener to Queen Caroline, Consort of George II. Official records recount that in 1726 'the Bason [sic] next to the Snailery was to be enlarged for Tortices' and to be 'raised so as to hold water 30 feet deep with a fence between the snailery and the tortoise place'. One can only speculate as to whether the occupants of these places were curiosities of natural history or intended for the palace menus!

The Serpentine, also seen in Edwardian days when nursemaids and their charges made up a large proportion of the park's visitors. The creation of the Serpentine, or Long Water, in 1730–1 was an enormous and costly enterprise involving vast excavations to transform pools in the Westbourne River into a lake. The bridge in the distance was built in 1826.

The Broad Walk (looking south, *c.* 1900) was also the creation of Charles Bridgeman. Fifty feet wide, leading from Kensington Gore to Bayswater Road, it became a fashionable promenade when the Gardens were opened to the public on Saturdays in the reign of George II when the court was at Kew. By the time of William IV they were open all the year round to 'respectably dressed persons'. In the 1930s the felling of the avenue of elm trees caused a public outcry.

Sheep were a familiar sight grazing in Kensington Gardens in the years both before and after the First World War. These four-legged lawn-mowers, with a phlegmatic attitude towards dogs, gave the park a pleasantly rural atmosphere.

KENSAL AND NORTH KENSINGTON

When this aerial photograph of North Kensington and Kensal Green was taken in 1935 the

area had probably reached the peak of its industrialization. Only the monuments in the

cemetery of All Souls (bottom left) provide a corner of tranquillity along the snaking course

of the Grand Union Canal. Railway lines, sidings and engine sheds fill the foreground,

with the Gas Light and Coke Company's gasometer towering above their newly-built

Kensal House flats, an experiment in working-class housing using gas power, with commu-

nal facilities such as a nursery and laundry. Large-scale slum clearance had only just

begun. By a curious quirk of medieval land ownership, much of the area known as Kensal

Town actually belonged to the parish of Chelsea until 1900.

Kensal Green gas works in 1909, some half a century after the Western Gas Company had established their first works there in 1845, on land isolated by the east–west lines of the canal and the Great Western Railway. The gas works expanded westward until they occupied all the land west of Ladbroke Grove.

This gas worker with his horse and cart was photographed in 1907.

The Victorian 'North Pole' public house on the corner of Latimer and North Pole Roads, seen here in 1910. It replaced an earlier one-storey country inn of the same name, and earlier still The Globe, probably dating from about 1839 when the Hippodrome race course reached to this point. Until the 1860s the area was completely rural, first used for training horses as the Notting Hill Hunting Grounds, then for market gardens. Among the early developments was a terrace of cottages called the 'Sixteens', each with its pig sty and vegetable plot, but by the 1890s the area became known as Soapsud Island, owing to the large number of cottage laundries there. In this photo a watchful policeman and locals, with two ale delivery draymen, pose for the photographer.

Kensington Public Baths and Wash Houses on the corner of Lancaster and Silchester Roads, seen here in 1900 (above), were opened in 1888. The need for laundry facilities by a community where few homes had laid-on water is clear from the statistics – nearly 60,000 women used the laundry in 1897. Equally important was the opportunity to teach children to swim, and the London Swimming Association used the bath for their instruction programme, a session of which is shown below, *c.* 1898.

A cricket game in progress at St Charles College in St Charles Square in 1890. The college, founded in Bayswater by Dr Henry (later Cardinal) Manning in 1863 to provide a Catholic education for upper-class boys, was housed in this handsome building with its 140 foot tower. Damaged during the Second World War, it was demolished and the site used to build secondary schools.

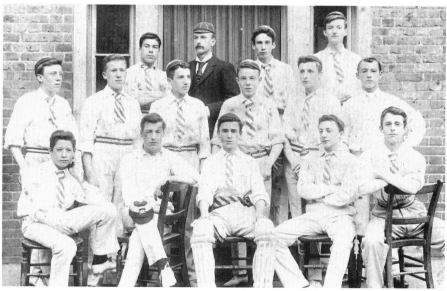

The Oxford Gardens School cricket team with their master, c. 1892–5. The school originated in 1884 when some of the leading local tradesmen petitioned the school board to provide state-aided education for their children, but at a fee high enough to keep out poorer families! Oxford Gardens was therefore a 'sixpenny school' until fees were abolished in 1891.

Talbot Mews at the turn of the century when these backways, intended to accommodate the carriages, horses and coachmen of the wealthy residents of the area, had deteriorated due to the developers' financial failures into a squalid mixture of cramped dwellings, sheds and workshops. They would have horrified the Talbot family for whom the mews was named. They had been owners of the farmland here since the early eighteenth century, and the Misses Mary-Anne and Georgina-Charlotte Talbot found themselves in Victorian days the inheritors not of mere fields but of land highly desirable for the building of houses and the laying of railway tracks. Those railways spelt the death of the mews in places such as Notting Hill where even comparatively wealthy residents in Ladbroke Grove dispensed with carriages in favour of the train. In Inner London the 'carriage trade' lasted much longer. So for several decades, until the advent of the motor car, the mews had no purpose except to house the poor in conditions which had never been salubrious. Living in close proximity to horses, with all the attendant sanitary problems, is not as romantic or amusing as later developers might have one believe.

Silchester Road in the 1900s was a busy shop-lined highway striking west from Lancaster Circus, the junction of Walmer, Lancaster and Clarendon Roads, to Latimer Road. In the 1960s it was chopped off near to its meeting with Bramley Road (below), most of which also succumbed to the bulldozers. Both roads were named for the Hampshire associations of their developer, James Whitchurch, a lawyer from Southampton.

Kenley Street (formerly William Street) in its last days before redevelopment in 1904. From the 1820s the arrival of the piggeries and potteries (brick-making) made the 'Dale' a slum. In 1904 Kenley Street was the scene of one of the first improvement schemes of the newly created Royal Borough. Active in both the planning and financing was Sir Henry Seymour King, the first mayor, who actually made a large interest-free loan of his own money so that the tumbled down properties could be bought. In the lower picture, Lady King is seen performing the opening ceremony (with the Mayor, Cllr J.P. Williams, on the left) on 8 November 1904, after the buildings had been refurbished, or demolished and rebuilt.

Two photographs of Crescent Street (now the site of Henry Dickens Court) in the 1930s, its last days before it was swept away in the borough's pre-war slum clearance plan. In 1893 a journalist writing in the *Daily News* described life there and in adjacent streets as 'these wretched places where life is more hopeless and degraded and abandoned than anything in London'. Together with neighbouring Bangor Street (famed for its rag fair) and Sirdar Road, Crescent Street was massively over-occupied with families of six or seven living in one room, or houses let as the lowest of lodgings where a bed on the floor cost a penny a night and sanitation was at its minimum.

This religious street procession celebrated the opening of St Columb's, the new High Anglican church in Lancaster Road, a mission church to neighbouring All Saints, in 1900. When the two churches amalgamated in 1951 the building became the Serbian Orthodox Church of St Sava.

Golborne Road, seen here in 1900, was intended for better things in a district called Portobello Park, but plans changed: the intended canal bridge never materialized and second-rate developers moved in.

Newspaper bill boards date this photograph of a shop front at Barton's newsagents, Lancaster Road, to 1912: 'Titanic Survivors', '200 Dead in Carpathia'. Daniel John Barton ran his tobacconist business at 161 Lancaster Road from 1909 to 1919. Lancaster Road was part of the widespread business interests of a famous – or infamous – Victorian property developer, Charles Henry Blake, whose later enterprises included not only house-building but investment in railways. Perhaps he sought to balance his more dubious activities by contributing to the foundation of no less than four churches in fifteen years – St John's on Ladbroke Hill, St Mark's, St Peter's in Kensington Park Road and St Michael and All Angels in Ladbroke Grove.

Ladbroke Grove in 1866, spanned by the new bridge of the Hammersmith and City railway opened only two years earlier, linking the area with the City via Paddington. Until then development in this northern end of the Grove had been sparse (as can be seen beyond the bridge) but now advertisements for the new houses could describe their 'most convenient situation' with speedy access to all parts of London for sixpence return!

Work proceeding on the new bridge in 1938 when it became the first all-welded steel plate girder bridge to be built in England. In the 1860s hundreds of imported navvies had built the first viaduct on this spot across the swampy land of Notting Dale.

Ladbroke Grove at its junction with Holland Park Avenue *c.* 1900 (above), when a horse-drawn cab rank awaited the requirements of the affluent residents who occupied the grand houses up to the crest of the hill. St John's Church spire can be seen in the distance. Just how affluent is made plain by the interior (below) of No. 42 Ladbroke Grove in 1915. These semi-detached houses were built *c.* 1845 as part of the scheme to create a neighbourhood comparable with Cheltenham or Regents Park.

Portobello Road *c*. 1900, when the street that was to become a tourist attraction sixty years later was still a line of homely shops, with the stalls confined to a small section, and selling mostly foodstuffs. In its earlier days the market functioned only on weekdays until the stallholders won over the Vestry to allow trading six days a week. Earlier still, Portobello Lane, which passed through fields of barley, was described as 'one of the pleasantest rural walks in London, with nothing to be heard in the tranquil silence but the notes of the lark, the linnet and the nightingale'.

A.J. Symons' newsagents and confectioners at No. 281 Portobello Road. The *Daily News* bill boards announcing the historic boxing match ('Carpentier's Defeat: Dramatic Scenes') date this photograph to 1924. Street betting was illegal but Racing Advice gives the tip for the day – Miss Megan 10 to 1. The business moved away in the early thirties.

Kensington Park Road on a sunny summer day, *c.* 1905, brings out the fashionable lady with her parasol and boater-hatted escort as they approach St Peter's Church near the junction of Stanley Gardens. Both streets were fashionable addresses in the Edwardian era. The novelist Katherine Mansfield and the man she eventually married, John Middleton Murry, lived at No. 95 Elgin Crescent. Kensington Park Road was the home of poster artist John Hassall for many decades, in a house later occupied by his equally talented daughter, Joan Hassall, and his son, the poet and lyricist Christopher Hassall.

Leafy Elgin Crescent on a postcard dated 1908 as a mother, or nanny, takes a chubby toddler for an afternoon walk.

This section of Westbourne Grove, near its junction with Kensington Park Road, seen here *c.* 1905, was known as Archer Street until comparatively recent times. It was named for G.S. Archer, the Kentish absentee landlord of the old 'Barley Shots' fields on which development began in the 1860s.

All Saints Road *c.* 1900, when Thomas's Dairy sold eggs at 8*d* a dozen and country milk direct from the farm, and before the street became infamous in the Rachmanism era of the 1950s and '60s.

An early twentieth-century view of the junction of Westbourne Grove with Pembridge Villas and Chepstow Road, once known as 'Bradley's Corner' (from the fashionable furriers on the corner of Chepstow Place). The early success of the area resulted largely from the foresight of its 1844 developers who laid nearly 5,000 feet of sewers to provide modern amenities for the attractive houses. The 1861 census reveals that most of the households in nearby Pembridge Gardens had at least three servants and the occupants included merchants, stockbrokers, surveyors and a colliery owner. In Pembridge Square the number of servants often exceeded that of the family itself with not only a cook, butler and lady's maid but a footman and page. The west end of Westbourne Grove, then known as Archer Street, was a shopping centre for these fashionable folk, the traders including a milliner, dressmaker, hairdresser, stay warehouse and clockmaker.

Section Three

NOTTING HILL

*Notting Hill Gate near the junction of Linden Gardens and the Mall in 1908, where only
the vintage vehicles date a scene which was to remain virtually unchanged until the brutal
redevelopment of the 1960s. Even now the north side retains the old shopfront lines and
Blands umbrella factory survived until the 1980s. The High Street was on the line of the
Roman road to Silchester, later known as 'the way to Uxbridge'. Even by the mid-eighteenth
century, with gravel pits on either side and only a cluster of houses, it hardly merited the
description of a village. The 'Gate' originated from the toll gate set up by the Turnpike
Trust, situated approximately at the present junction with Pembridge Road, an unpopular
institution only removed in 1864. It was not until the coming of the Metropolitan 'Circle
Line' railway in 1868, that its transformation into a shopping centre began.*

The north side of Notting Hill Gate *c.* 1900, showing The Plough, the Victorian successor of an ancient coaching inn, and the shop terrace which was demolished in the 1960s to provide the site for Campden Hill Towers.

This 1905 view of Notting Hill Gate looks west from the junction with Ossington Street (on the right) with the Champion public house and Wellington Terrace. The latter was a row of shops which originated when the building of the Metropolitan Railway led to redevelopment, sweeping away the tumbled down cottages of Campden Place in the 1870s.

The Coronet Theatre, Notting Hill Gate, at the height of its splendour in Edwardian days when its stage was graced by stars such as Henry Irving. Converted to a cinema in 1921, it was saved from demolition in the 1980s by public campaigns.

On 1 February 1918 Princess Louise, Duchess of Argyll, visited the Coronet Theatre to inaugurate Kensington's War Savings week. She is seen here being received by (left to right) Mr Austin Chamberlain, Lord Claud Hamilton, MP for South Kensington, and the Mayor of Kensington, Sir William Davison.

Linden Gardens in 1907 retained much of the leafy charm it had in its early Victorian days when it was known as Linden Grove. Among its famous residents were two artists, the Royal Academician Thomas Creswick and William Mulready. It was here that Mulready designed the first penny postage envelope depicting Britannia sending out messages world wide. When Thomas Creswick moved from 42 Linden Grove into Mulready's house in 1866 it was taken by the actor Alfred Wigan and was used for the wedding reception of Sir Henry Irving.

The Central Line station at Notting Hill Gate, the 'Twopenny Tube', shortly after its opening in 1900. The first tube railway of the modern type, it ran from Shepherds Bush to the Bank for the flat fare of twopence, hence its nickname.

The building of the Metropolitan Railway station at Notting Hill Gate in 1868 (above) when the line was extended from Paddington to South Kensington via Bayswater and Notting Hill, using tunnels under many of the newly-built houses. Below, as the station appeared in 1905. When its first section from Farringdon Street to Paddington opened five years earlier it was the first underground railway in the world. In the 1950s it was demolished and replaced by an underground concourse linking access to the Metropolitan, Inner Circle, District and Central lines.

The junction of Pembridge Road with Notting Hill Gate in 1905. The Edwardian fashions, a horse-drawn delivery van and handcarts turn back the clock on the building line that is practically the same today, although the traders have changed. On the opposite side of the street (below) there is a different story: a modern block has replaced Barnham and Marriages, tea and coffee importers, Adams Butchers and Goodmans Teeth, with a W.H. Smith – only the Prince Albert remains.

Norland Square, seen here at the beginning of the twentieth century, was the darling of its developer, the wealthy solicitor Charles Richardson, in the 1840s. He lived there himself, at No. 29, arranging for the maintenance of the garden, street repair and cleaning, and mains water, as he did with his other interests, St James Gardens and Royal Crescent. The aerial view (below) shows the latter, with the roller skating rink (the site of which is now a Hilton Hotel) in the foreground.

Horse buses in Holland Park Avenue at the turn of the century (above) share the highway with a cyclist as two little boys idle their way to school. In the same road at roughly the same date (below), looking north towards Notting Hill Gate from the entrance of Campden Hill Square, a nanny keeps up a brisk pace with her charges as elegant ladies stroll behind.

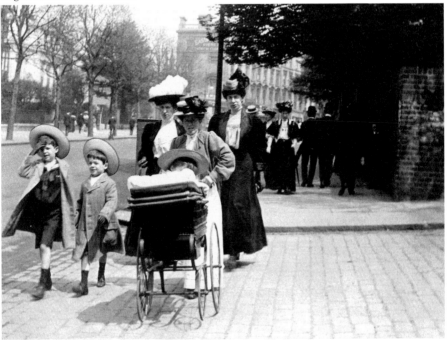

Holland Park in its Edwardian heyday – its magnificence still hardly altered since it was built in the 1860s. 'Good and substantial dwellings' was the insistence of its owner, Lord Holland, to the developer 'and all large trees to be preserved'. Some idea of their size and elegance is given by the view (below) of the garden at the rear of No. 80 in which their developer, William Radford, once lived with his family.

One of the last of the old shops in Uxbridge Street to go in recent times was Wittekind's, the bakers, in family ownership since its founders, Adam and Teresa Wittekind, came from Germany in Victorian times. They are seen here with their staff in 1906.

Not far from the Wittekind's shop was Dartmouth Street (now Hillgate Place), which shared the reputation of its neighbour, Johnson Street (now Hillgate Street), as 'a dingy ill-favoured slum', according to the vicar of St George's Church who appealed for the relief of its inhabitants. It is seen here in 1906.

Times were changing – forty years or more separate this picture (above) of workmen employed by J.P. Williams, the builders and decorators, at work on a Notting Hill villa in 1920 and that (below) where the old shops and cottages on the north-west corner of Kensington Church Street were being demolished in 1879 to make way for the building of the new Board school, itself later demolished in the 1950s for the Notting Hill redevelopment. (J. P. Williams, builders, were established at 87 Lancaster Road *c.* 1890 and continued in business until the mid-1960s.)

Bullingham Mansions in Kensington Church Street *c.* 1903, with a carriage waiting outside. The flats were built in 1894 on the site of the house where it is popularly supposed Sir Isaac Newton lived his last years. On the east side of Church Street was glebe land of the vicar of Kensington (land assigned to the incumbent as part of his benefice) and until 1877, when it moved further to the east, a vicarage was situated at the junction with Vicarage Gate. In 1954 the Church Commissioners purchased the freehold, apart from the vicar's house and garden. Winchester Court was built in 1935 on the site, previously occupied by a large house which was converted into a convent in 1851 and later became the Orphanage of St Vincent de Paul.

This view as Church Street goes downhill towards the High Street shows the Roman Catholic Carmelite church on the right (destroyed in the Second World War and rebuilt), and in the distance the newly-built spire of St Mary Abbots, *c.* 1879. When Father Herman (Cohen), a Jewish convert to Catholicism, came to London in 1862 he rented a house in Church Street on the site of today's Newton Court. In 1865 he bought the land opposite for £3,500 on which the Church of Our Lady of Mount Carmel and St Simon Stock was built. Ten years later, the community extended its land to the west and it was here that the Carmelite Monastery (an enclosed order) was built in 1886, connected to the church by a corridor.

Section Four

HOLLAND PARK AND CAMPDEN HILL

Holland House c. 1900, the stately home of historic families since Jacobean times when the

extravagant mansion was known as 'Cope's Castle'. It was created for Sir Walter Cope, one

of the richest men in the land, property dealer, entrepreneur and money-lender; it went on to

become the home of the turncoat Henry Rich, Earl of Holland. Although he lost his head in

the Civil War the house remained in his family's possession until the eighteenth century,

when it was the hub of social and political life in the ownership of the Fox family. It had

seen drama, intrigue, romance and scandal in an elegant setting until the night of 27/28

September 1940 when it was disastrously damaged during an air raid. At one time it

seemed this was the end but a vigorous campaign of public opinion saved what was left.

The east wing was restored as the King George VI Memorial Youth Hostel, and the

extensive grounds became one of the most attractive public parks in London.

The West Room of Holland House in 1886 when it had become the home of Lord Ilchester, a distant relative of the Fox family, and once again became the scene of balls, garden parties and lavish entertainment, in a setting of sedate opulence.

At about the same time, gardeners with a donkey-drawn mower tend the lawn outside the garden ballroom. The ballroom (now the Belvedere Restaurant) was converted from the granary in 1849; it was reached from the house by the cloistered walk and terrace above, and was adjacent to the orangery, now a venue for concerts and art shows.

It would be hard to convince today's occupants of Oakwood Court, Addison Road, that the extensive gardens and lake of Oak Lodge, seen here in 1894, stood on the site of their flats at 25 Addison Road. The site of the house had been bought from the Holland estate in the 1850s and sold again in 1862 to James McHenry who extended its grounds, making the lake out of the Old Moats fishponds of Holland House. In 1873 he offered to buy the whole of the Hollands' remaining estate from Lady Holland, who was in serious financial difficulties from both her lavish lifestyle and the maintenance of the property, but she instead passed the inheritance over to Lord Ilchester, who would in any case have received it on her death, and the beautiful remnant of another age was preserved. A plate on the wall of 13 Melbury Road inscribed 'J McH 1877' marks the boundary of McHenry's land, which in its turn was sold for the building of Oakwood Court in 1900. St Barnabas Church, consecrated in 1829, can be seen in the background.

In 1906 Holland Walk was as popular with young mothers and their babies as it is today, although fashions have changed in perambulators. A right of way since 1848, it has sometimes been disputed but has endured, despite threats of closure, or conversion to a traffic highway.

Duchess of Bedford Walk in 1930 when it was still no more than a leafy byway leading from Holland Walk between the boundary fences of secluded villas to Bedford Lodge, home of the Duke and Duchess of Bedford from 1823 to 1853. Bedford Lodge, later renamed Cam House, was demolished in 1955.

The site of Bute House, seen above in 1912, is now largely covered by the Queen Elizabeth College on Campden Hill. Built in 1812, its first resident was Richard Gillow, probably a member of the cabinet makers Waring and Gillow, but its name commemorated a later occupant (1830–42), the Marquess of Bute. The University of London took a 999-year lease of the site in 1914, after the house had been demolished, for its Kings College women's department. The college, now renamed for Queen Elizabeth II, also swallowed up neighbouring Thornwood Lodge in 1956. The picture below shows the site during demolition.

Lord Leighton (1830–96), the Victorian artist *par excellence*, whose first Royal Academy painting (bought by the Queen) was hung when he was twenty-five, and who became President of the Royal Academy in 1878. His friendship with the fourth Lord Holland, which brought him often to Holland House, obviously inspired his choice of Kensington for the house which he envisaged as 'meeting the needs of a working painter with a lofty studio'. 'I am indeed truly sorry to hear of Lord Holland's death,' he wrote to his mother in 1859. 'Nothing could exceed his kindness to me.'

Five years later he obtained a 99-year lease from Lady Holland for the site in Holland Park Road to build his dream home, designed by his friend, George Aitchison. This view of the entrance hall in 1897 shows that despite his desire for a working home, he ornamented it with exotic décor, tiling and stained glass. Leighton House was much smaller as first planned in 1866 (only one bedroom was included in the plan to discourage guests who might interrupt the artist's work!), and the famous Arab Hall, intended to display his marvellous collection of tiles, was not created until 1877.

No black and white photograph can convey the extraordinary wealth of colour in the black and gold lacquered woodwork and ornate furnishings of Leighton House, seen here *c.* 1890s. It was the work of such contemporaries as Walter Crane, William De Morgan and Randolph Caldecott. After Leighton's death in 1896 several attempts were made to purchase the house for the nation, but it was not until 1926 that the freehold was acquired by Kensington Borough Council. It is now open free of charge to the public as well as being used for various exhibitions and concerts.

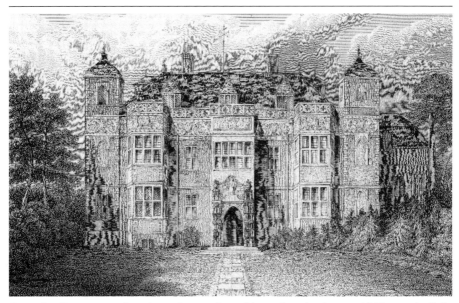

Campden House, seen here in an impression of its early splendour *c*. 1800, was built in 1612 for Baptist Hicks, later Viscount Campden, who as a city financier 'knew how to amass money and spend it'. The estate is bounded today by Sheffield Terrace, Hornton Street and Kensington Church Street. When Viscount Campden died in 1629 he left £200 for the poor of Kensington; as the Campden Charities, this has grown into many millions and benefited innumerable good causes.

His descendants retained the house until 1708 when it was sold and used as a girls' boarding school, seen here in an early lithograph which gives some idea of its lavish décor.

In 1691 Campden House was let for a while to Princess (later Queen) Anne and Prince George of Denmark. Returning to private occupation its residents included Mr William Wolley, who built a private theatre there in which Charles Dickens acted in *The Lighthouse* in 1854. Then disaster struck: in 1862 the house was burned down. The photograph shows fire officials surveying the gutted ruins. Although a similar, and perhaps even more ornate, house took its place, it had a short life and was demolished in 1900. The site was used to build Campden House Court flats.

Hornton Street, shortly before this terrace was demolished in 1903 and replaced by the present houses on the east side. This area is on the Phillimore estate, in the ownership of the family of that name since the early eighteenth century. The west side of Hornton Street kept the charm of its earlier life until the new town hall was built in 1972, for here was the Red House, later occupied by Herbert Hoover, who became President of the USA and who described it as 'a house with a quaint garden in the middle of a great city'. Its next-door neighbour, Niddry Lodge, was named for its second occupant in the 1840s, the Dowager Countess of Hopetown, whose husband, the 5th Earl, was also Baron Niddry.

Sir James South (1785–1867), the astronomer who bought the mansion which had once been the home of the Phillimores in 1827, constructing an observatory in the garden. Throughout his residence he refused to allow a road to be built near his house for fear that the vibration from traffic would interfere with his astronomical observances; Campden Hill Road was only opened at its southern end in 1867 after his death. He is seen here in the 1860s with his dog, Tiger.

HOLLAND STREET, KENSINGTON.

Holland Street in 1909, when its traders included a dairy, a tailor's and a cycle shop. Known as Parsons Yard in the eighteenth century, it was a public way leading from Church Street to Holland House.

The building of Holland Street began as early as 1724 and continued throughout the next century, and in 1846 a developer built two houses on one of the remaining vacant plots, one of which, No. 15, was occupied by the poet Jean Ingelow (1820–97) (right). The site is now a block of flats named after her. The west side of this faces Kensington Church Walk, which had existed as a cartway to the parsonage since at least 1726. In 1767 the vicar agreed to allow the Vestry to make it a public pathway through the churchyard, but it was not extended to Kensington High Street until 1914.

Tower Cressy in 1930, the fanciful folly built in Aubrey Road, on Campden Hill, by the Victorian engineer Thomas Page, the year after the opening of the Great Exhibition in 1852–3. It survived until hit by a flying bomb during the Second World War, and was then demolished. Thomas Page, who built Westminster Bridge and the Albert Embankment, intended his romantic castle home to be a tribute to the Black Prince, whose emblems appeared on each storey above the arched doorway. Dr Christopher Dresser, the decorative designer, lived here with his wife and thirteen children between 1869 and 1882.

Section Five

KENSINGTON HIGH STREET

St Mary Abbots Church in 1860, a few years before the late seventeenth-century building

was demolished, an event which marked the end of the 'village' character of old Kensington.

The 'High Street' was becoming too narrow for the increasing traffic and there were

constant complaints about its poor lighting. The handsome new Vestry Hall nearby

provided a striking contrast to the shabby church, which, although rebuilt in 1696, had a

history of constant repair, possibly due to undermining by the vaults still below it, or

Kensington's unstable gravel soil. There had been a church on the site since medieval times,

and although the old tower had been retained it had to be replaced in 1722. The growing

population was also putting an enormous physical strain on the structure, said in one report

to be visibly bulging, and in 1866 it was declared unsafe with dry rot in the beams.

Demolition began in 1869 and Sir George Gilbert Scott was appointed architect of the

church as we know it today.

This must be one of the last photographs of the old church before its demise, showing the west front and tower in 1865. Its end was controversial, criticized as extravagance by some people and as being undertaken not a day too soon by others. The *Kensington News*, for instance, declared that 'if something was not done quickly the voice of prayer would be changed to cries of terror as its frequenters were buried beneath its ruins'!

On Ascension Day 1869 the church held its last services. A few days before the demolition began the Cumberland Society rang a farewell on the bells, a ten-part peal of grandsire triples. This was followed by another marathon peal on the anniversary of the Queen's coronation; the bells were taken down the following day, 29 June 1869.

On 14 May 1872 the new church was consecrated – though without its landmark spire. This photograph was taken some weeks earlier when the site was still sealed off and the churchyard gate taken over by flyposters advertising *Sporting Opinion* and other racing journals! The spire, the highest in London and the sixth highest in England, was not completed until 1879, and the south porch and cloisters until 1893. The final stone of the spire was laid by the vicar, the Revd the Hon. Edward Carr Glyn who, with twelve parishioners, two church wardens and a correspondent of *The Times*, climbed the scaffolding by a series of ladders and held a service 264 feet above the crowd below. It was a blustery day and *The Times* reported that the scaffolding was swaying 'slightly but perceptibly in the wind'. Mr Carr Glyn nevertheless laid the capstone safely in position and blessed the 14 foot metal cross.

These new bells were added to the peal in 1879. They bear the inscription 'Those evening bells, how many a tale their music tells' and (the smaller bell) 'Invite. Warn. Rejoice. Mourn.' Standing proudly by are (left to right) Mr Reuben Green, vestry clerk, and Mr Robert Henry Pearson and Mr Jubal Webb, church wardens, whose names are also engraved on the bells.

The 278 foot spire houses the peal of ten bells, on which the church clock chimes the hours and quarters, although there is no visible clock face because it was thought it might spoil the look of the spire. The invisible clock mechanism was exhibited at the Universal Exhibition in 1862. In this picture, dated 1892, intrepid steeplejacks can be seen carrying out repairs on the spire. Of the older bells, some had already been recast in 1772 and some had to be recast in 1872. Among the inscriptions on these is the curiously pagan reference 'The ringers' art our grateful notes prolong, Apollo listens and approves the song'. The ringers' art is often heard from the belfry and celebration peals have been rung on occasions such as royal births.

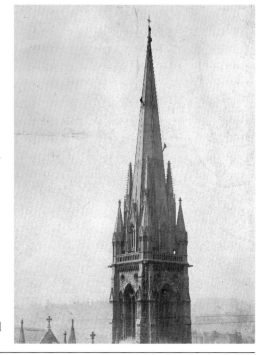

St Mary Abbots School, Group I, in 1900 (above), with their teacher Miss Jewell. This photograph was supplied to Kensington and Chelsea Libraries by Walter Brown, who is seen next to her (in a sailor suit). His father was a coachman and the other children all come from local tradesmen's families. The school met at the Mission Hall in South End. The school in 1924 (left) appears much as it does today, including the painted wooden figures of a boy and girl which have decorated its entrance for nearly 300 years. The school has its roots in the days of Queen Anne, occupying a building designed by Nicholas Hawksmoor in the High Street in 1711, until the Victorian Town Hall took the site in 1871.

In 1880 Kensington Vestry Hall still retained much of the splendour of the time of its building some thirty years earlier in 1851 when ratepayers had complained of its extravagant embellishments such as gilded railings and chandeliers. Until then the Vestry men had met in the parish room. After the building of the Town Hall in 1880 the railings and gate piers were moved, and in 1889 it became the central library. With the creation of the new library in 1960, it was taken over by the Melli Bank.

13th London Regiment (Princess Louise' Kensington Regiment) parading outside Kensington Town Hall on 9 August 1914, five days after the declaration of the First World War, and handing over the regimental colours to the mayor, Sir William Davison MP, for safe custody before leaving for France. There they suffered terrible losses in the early years of the 'Old Contemptibles'.

The first scaffolding goes up in 1905 for the building of Hornton Court (above). The demolition reveals 'The Abbey', the eccentric Gothic folly built by William Abbot in Victorian times which, after extensive air raid damage in the Second World War, became the site of the new library. The architect of Hornton Court, built in 1907 (seen below), was Frank Sydney Chesterton, of Chesterton and Sons, a relation of the famous G.K. Chesterton. Frank Chesterton died in action in the First World War.

Chesterton's premises on the corner of Campden Hill Road and the High Street in 1909. The family firm had links with the Phillimore family, and this section of Lower Phillimore Place survived until 1931 when it too was redeveloped as modern flats, Phillimore Court.

Holland Park Dairy in its last days, *c.* 1914. As Holland House estate became more built up, the owners of Holland Park Farm were allowed to build a new dairy and cow sheds on the corner of Melbury Road. Although the cows left, the building, which was designed to match the nearby lodge houses, survived in use as a United Dairies shop until the 1960s redevelopment.

The 'big cheese' (in every sense) of Victorian Kensington must be Jubal Webb, the cheesemonger, whose shop was already well established next to St Mary Abbots Church in 1869. Flamboyant, publicity-seeking, entrepreneur, leading vestryman and church warden, his telegraphic address was Gorgonzola, London. He is seen here with the giant cheese he exhibited at the Chicago World Fair in 1893, which weighed 207,250 pounds! In 1886 Jubal Webb moved to The Terrace (now 129–61 Kensington High Street) which ran from Wrights Lane to Adam and Eve Mews. Dating from 1690, its residents included Henry Cole, William Banting, the dietician, and artists David Wilkie and John Leech. In 1892 Webb bought the whole four and a quarter acre estate, presented a strip of the frontage to the Vestry to widen the road, and built Iverna Gardens behind.

Gardeners Buildings, seen here in its last days *c.* 1865, was one of the tumbled down yards in Market Court which originated in the 1770s behind the frontage of the High Street. They were all swept away by improvements and road widening in the 1870s. Despite its appearance, this court was not as notorious for evil living conditions as the other rookery buildings further east, notably Jennings Buildings. The 1851 census shows that over half of its residents were Irish, mostly from County Cork. Their occupations were typical and included 62 labourers, 58 women who worked in the neighbouring market gardens, 27 laundresses and 28 washerwomen (though one doubts, given the appalling sanitary conditions, how they managed to ply their trade) and 44 street traders. The area was condemned by all but neither the Vestry nor the negligent landlord took action.

From 1889 the big Kensington stores, Barker's, Derry & Tom's and Ponting's, had to compete with Pettit's and W.H. Hunt & Co. on the corner of the High Street and Allen Street, seen here in 1900. In 1919 Barker's, who wished to expand, offered £40,000 for Hunt's but were refused. The shop closed in 1923 when The Terrace was redeveloped, apart from the corner premises which can still be identified.

In 1923 the site of the Odeon Cinema was still Leonard's Place, an early nineteenth-century development. First to go were the houses removed for the premises of carriage builders which later became the motor sales and works of Strachan and Brown and then, in 1924, the Kensington Cinema was built, the largest cinema in England, seating 2,350 people. This later became the Majestic and then the Odeon.

In 1920, before the drastic reconstruction of the store which changed the whole face of the High Street, Barker's Tea Room, with potted plants and uniformed waitresses, served 'New Jersey sundaes' for a shilling to summer shoppers.

The Town Hall Tavern, seen here in 1890, was built in 1871 on land surplus to the building of the station. Known originally as the Duke of Abercorn, it survived until 1912 and the expansion of Derry & Tom's. The gateway on the right led to Francis Tucker & Co., the famous Roman Catholic family of candlemakers, whose factory was situated behind this frontage (the chimney can be seen on the right), where it had been since the 1760s. Although going into voluntary liquidation in 1908, their name was retained by Price's, who took the business over. The archway next to Tucker's became the entrance to a Lyon's tea shop.

Work began on Kensington High Street station in 1865 and the enormous 90 foot wide roof span seen here was completed two years later. The arrival of the trains set the seal on the High Street's potential as one of London's most popular shopping centres. The area to the west of the station was the home from 1821 to 1835 of William Cobbett, the radical journalist, who set off from here on his famous 'Rural Rides'.

In 1909 times were changing in the High Street, especially on the south side. Some of the businesses here, such as Keith Prowse, survived in new premises, but by the 1960s most of the terrace was taken over by Kensington Market.

The north side of Kensington High Street in the 1880s (above), where a variety of buildings and traders provided an interesting row of shops from photographic studios to provision stores. Decorations for Queen Victoria's Golden Jubilee in 1887 (right) enliven the Duke of Cumberland, Wells the jeweller's and a florist's. The whole of this side of the High Street was demolished for road widening in 1903 and advertised as a building site by the Crown Commissioners, but there were no buyers, despite early suggestions for a cinema.

Kensington House, seen here in 1880 at the end of its short life. This magnificent mansion, situated roughly on the site of Kensington Court, built to replace two earlier grand houses, was the flamboyant creation for the Victorian financier and entrepreneur Albert Grant. Begun in 1873 the grand edifice, surrounded by extensive grounds, with a lake, bowling alley and skating rink, boasted twenty bedrooms, ballroom, banqueting room, winter and summer dining rooms, billiard room, huge conservatory and grand hall, and numerous other facilities. It was completed by 1876 but Grant never occupied it, and it was eventually put up for sale, possibly as a club or a college, and finally demolished in 1882.

The Kensington toll gate, situated on Kensington Road near the junction with Palace Gate, seen here in its last days in the 1860s.

Section Six

CENTRAL KENSINGTON

Young Street in the 1890s, at its junction with Kensington High Street, is one of the oldest
side streets in Kensington, having been laid out in 1685 when it was the only entrance to
Kensington Square. It was named after the square's developer, Thomas Young. Sadly,
hardly anything remains of the original seventeenth-century houses, occupied by courtiers
and high-ranking soldiers in the retinue of William of Orange, as well as by tradesmen and
shopkeepers who also served the royal household. In this it encapsulates much of the
Kensington and Chelsea story, the way in which the fancy of the rich and fashionable gave
birth to a community to support their needs.

William Makepeace Thackeray (1811–63) took No. 16 Young Street (the house third from the left with a bow window) in 1846 and it was here that he wrote *Vanity Fair* and *Esmond*. At that time the street was still largely unchanged, but from 1860 wholesale alterations began and have never ceased, although often in the face of local opposition. The corner of Young Street and the High Street (see p. 83) was occupied in 1894 by the greengrocer, Slater, but demolition had already begun as part of the redevelopment of the main road. The corner site is now a bank.

Thackeray's first taste of domestic happiness was found at 16 Young Street, where he lived with his young daughters after many years of separation (the family was broken up because of his wife's insanity, the little girls being cared for by their grandparents in Paris). His joy in this reunion is apparent when he wrote happily about his new home, 'Kensington Gardens at the gate and omnibuses every two minutes. What can a mortal want more?' He stayed there nearly ten years, moving to Onslow Square in 1855 and finally to Palace Green, where he died in 1863. The photograph on the right was taken shortly before his death at 2 Palace Green.

These stalwarts represent about three-quarters of Kensington's fire brigade in the 1860s, photographed with their new engine after attending a fire in Lower Phillimore Mews. In 1871 the Board of Works reserved a site on the corner of Ball Street (a new, short-lived shopping street connecting Young Street and King Street – now Derry Street) parallel with the High Street, to build a new fire station with accommodation for three married men, three single men, one driver, three horses and three engines. The station closed in 1906 when a new fire station was built in Old Court Place. Within a few years, in 1912, the firemen and colleagues from many other parts of London were called to a disastrous fire at Barker's expanded premises across the road, when five staff members died. Ball Street was swallowed up in a further expansion of Barker's in 1927.

Dr John Merriman (1826–96), a member of a famous nineteenth-century medical family which occupied No. 45 Kensington Square for over half a century. The house backed on to that occupied by Thackeray, with adjoining gardens, and the story of the two homes is curiously linked. John Merriman was an historian and pioneer photographer, and his records of his neighbourhood in mid-Victorian times have provided a unique archive, all of which he bequeathed to Kensington Libraries, an invaluable visual aid to researchers. This photograph was taken *c.* 1870s.

Volunteers working for the war supply depot set up at Nos 11, 12 and 13 Kensington Square, here photographed rolling bandages in 1917. They also produced splints, slings and other surgical aids and dressings from material donated by the public. A report of the depot states, 'Were it not for such work the wounded would have no recovery.'

The west side of Kensington Square, *c.* 1900. The largest house here, No. 27, was occupied from the 1830s to the 1890s by the Kensington Proprietary Grammar School for Boys. When its fortunes began to fade, the back garden was taken to build the railway, and eventually the whole site was sold to the Crown and let to Derry & Tom's, who already had other houses in the square for staff accommodation. An archway was cut through No. 25 to allow vehicles to reach a warehouse.

The Convent of the Assumption in Kensington Square *c.* 1900, with girls of the junior school playing cricket – surprisingly progressive for Edwardian days. The community of nuns of the Order of the Assumption took the houses in the south-western corner of the square in 1859, adding a chapel in 1870–5. They established several schools and, in modern times, a teacher training college.

Woolsthorpe House in Wrights Lane became a 'home for crippled boys' in 1869. Built in the late eighteenth century, it was enlarged after being taken over by a charity which intended to educate, board and clothe destitute, ill-used or neglected disabled boys. The site was sold in 1935 and the proceeds used to provide a college at Stanmore. It has now become Kensington Close Hotel. In this picture the inmates in the early 1900s are enjoying a game of football despite their disabilities.

Britannia Brewery in Allen Street, shortly before its demolition in 1928. Note the imposing figure of Britannia on its roof. It was built in 1834 by Edward Herington and William Wells, with its attached pub the Britannia Tap (which survives in modern guise), but after various financial crises it finally closed in 1924.

St Mary Abbots Hospital in Marloes Road (above *c.* 1900) began its life as the parish workhouse. In 1846 a small infirmary was included, and this was gradually enlarged until a new building was created in 1871, and the chapel of St Elizabeth in 1874 (below *c.* 1800). Extensions continued over the next sixty years, during which time the LCC took over the hospital and the workhouse closed. The buildings suffered severe damage during the Second World War. It was closed under the reorganization of London hospitals in the 1980s, and the site redeveloped for housing.

South End, which lies behind the south side of Kensington Square, seen here in 1900, had probably changed little since it had served as stabling for the wealthy residents of the neighbourhood a century earlier. At that time the beautiful 'Spring Gardens' and bowling green, laid out at great expense by the builder, Thomas Young, in the 1680s, had been 'digged up' to his consternation and sorrow by his successor, sold off as market gardens and later built upon. Garages replaced stables before its 'prettification' in present times.

Victoria Grove in Edwardian times, some sixty years after its construction as part of the fashionable Kensington New Town (1837–43). It was created on the estate of a wealthy importer of pipes and snuff, John Inderwick, and was earlier part of the manor of Earls Court, known as Towney Meads.

Cottesmore Gardens, a terrace of considerably varied houses, seen here *c.* 1919, was built a half-century or so earlier. The tower of the Imperial Institute can be seen in the distance.

The fashions of the early 1920s smilingly displayed by residents of No. 24 Cottesmore Gardens, from a family photo album inscribed 'E.G. Hunter of Kent House, Kensington Court'.

The cul-de-sac Kensington Gate (off Gloucester Road) in the 1920s, when Barker's delivered bread daily by horse-drawn cart. This too was on the land of John Inderwick, whose firm lives on in Carnaby Street.

The Gloucester Arms, Gloucester Road, in 1903. The pub still flourishes on the corner of Victoria Grove. It was first occupied by Thomas Hitchcock in 1839. St George's Terrace on the opposite side of the junction only changed from its Victorian guise in 1907, when the row of houses with front gardens on the west side of Gloucester Road was demolished to build the present St George's Court with shops below.

Gloucester Road station nearing its completion in 1868. The station was shared by the Metropolitan and District Railway, and in 1906 excavations were undertaken to construct the Piccadilly Line beneath it.

Bailey's Hotel, next to the station, was commenced in 1875 as the most ambitious venture to date by James Bailey, a businessman from Norfolk who lived there for a time with his family. The hotel was built to the highest standards of amenity to attract American visitors. (Note the bath chair and its attendant in the foreground.)

'Cab, Sir?' Queens Gate Terrace, where hansoms await customers in 1900. This and other developments in the vicinity were undertaken in the 1850s by the Broadwood family, the famous makers of keyboard instruments and pianos.

Queens Gate (originally known as Prince Albert's Road) as envisaged in 1853 by the area's main developer, William Jackson, whose grandiose mansions stretch westwards, away from the open country towards London. Jackson had his difficulties and nearly went bankrupt in the late 1850s.

Section Seven

SOUTH KENSINGTON AND THE MUSEUMS

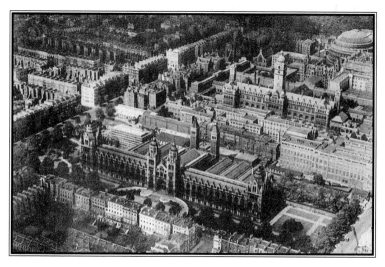

The museums area of South Kensington, a 1930s aerial view taken from the south-east with

the Royal Albert Hall in the distance (right). The area is in some ways as much a memorial

to the Prince Consort as the monument which bears his name, for it was the surplus funds

from the 1851 Great Exhibition which helped to create this district devoted to the promotion

of the arts and sciences. The Commissioners of the Exhibition were to spend the next ten

years planning the complex of institutions which eventually filled the area around Cromwell

and Exhibition Roads and Queens Gate. First to be established after the acquisition of the

estate, which was to cover 87 acres, was the South Kensington Museum, or Iron Museum,

in temporary buildings nicknamed the Brompton Boilers for their unprepossessing

appearance. This became the Victoria and Albert Museum, but not for fifty years.

The Royal Albert Hall seen from the park, *c.* 1900. When Queen Victoria attended the opening in 1871, she found the occasion very moving, for the idea of such a venue for the performance of music had been dear to Prince Albert's heart and cherished by his (and later the Queen's) private secretary, General Charles Grey, who also died before he could see the dream fulfilled. Arguments over its building and the necessary finance were protracted but eventually resulted in the building of today with its magnificent mosaic frieze of Grecian figures.

This engraving in the *Stationers' Almanac* of 1870 envisages the Memorial to Prince Albert two years before its inauguration, after years of debate on its nature, detail and setting. The Prince sits in effigy (though now shrouded by scaffolding) under the ornate castellated canopy with its mosaic decorations, a copy of the catalogue of the Great Exhibition of 1851 in his hand.

Exhibition grounds in 1872. In 1869 the Commissioners announced a series of exhibitions linking art, science and commerce, held in new galleries which stretched north and south on either side of a central garden.

These ornate gardens of the Royal Horticultural Society, seen here in 1872, attracted thousands of visitors every year to the 20 acre site south-west of the Royal Albert Hall between 1861 and 1880. It is almost impossible today to imagine that huge area of arcades, topiary, mosaic pavements and statues, now built over.

This view of Brompton Park House painted by R. Collinson in 1865 shows the International Exhibition building, demolished at the end of 1864, towering behind its garden trees. The famous gardener, Henry Wise, had taken it in 1698, and successive residents lavished care and attention upon it. Although the new museum grew around it, the house itself survived to be used as a school of art, and was not demolished until 1899 when the Victoria and Albert Museum was constructed, as the photograph below, taken *c*. 1890s by Beatrix Potter's father, Rupert, shows.

Work in progress on the building of the new Victoria and Albert Museum in 1903 (above). In the forty years or so since its foundation the 'South Kensington Museum' had become a hotch-potch of buildings, among which were scattered the early collections, later acquisitions and educational departments. In the 1880s endless debates took place on its future and in 1890 architects competed to design a new building. The successful candidate was Sir Aston Webb, and in 1899 the foundation stone was laid by Queen Victoria. In June 1909 it was opened by King Edward VII. The photograph below shows it four years later, when today's plane trees were still saplings.

Onslow Square in the early 1900s. It was built between 1845 and 1865 on the estate left by Henry Smith, a wealthy seventeenth-century Alderman, as a charity 'to relieve the sufferings of Christians held in captivity by Turkish pirates', the Earl of Onslow being one of its trustees. An Act of Parliament later allowed it to be used for other charitable purposes. Among its past residents was William Makepeace Thackeray (see p. 84).

The west side of Cromwell Place in 1906 demonstrates the rivalry between the horse and the motor in public transport. This street, leading from South Kensington station to Cromwell Road, was developed by John Alexander, who had to wait until 1822 before he could build on much of the land owing to the leases on nursery gardens.

Sumner Place, seen here *c.* 1900, was also named for trustees of the Smith Charity estate (see p. 100), George and William Holme Sumner, and was known earlier as Sumner Terrace. In common with so much of this area, it was built up by Sir Charles James Freake, son of a coal merchant who became a builder/architect and used much of his large fortune to promote the arts and music and other public benefactions.

Onslow Gardens, seen here at the turn of the century, was among the later developments, but equally grand. In the 1871 census, when only twenty houses were occupied, there were 175 inhabitants of which over a hundred were servants. Famous residents included Andrew Bonar Law, Prime Minister from 1922 to 1923, and Sir Leslie Stephens, first editor of the *Dictionary of National Biography*.

The Imperial Institute seen from roof-top level in the autumn of 1903. The Institute was opened by Queen Victoria in May 1893, to 'present the Arts, Manufactures and Commerce of the Queen's Colonial and Indian Empire'. Designed by T.E. Collcutt, its 287 foot central tower was retained as a memorial when the rest of the Institute was demolished for the building of the new Imperial College in 1957–65.

Cromwell Gardens in its last years of private occupation, *c.* 1900. By 1914 the houses were sold off to the Office of Works, which leased them to the Institut Français. In 1937 the site was sold with the object of building a national theatre. Bernard Shaw launched the campaign in 1938 but it came to naught and the area remained vacant for many years.

Alexander Square, named for its fortunate young owner, John Alexander, who inherited an enormous Kensington estate from his godfather in 1799. When he died, his son, Henry Brown Alexander, continued its development. Although he and other landowners were happy to have the railway station, they were not so eager to have it situated on their land, and Alexander eventually had to convey a large number of houses to the railway company.

The Royal School of Needlework in Exhibition Road in 1905. The school was founded in 1872, with the purpose of reviving the art of decorative embroidery, by Princess Christian of Schleswig Holstein, third daughter of the Queen. It moved to this impressive site in 1903. In 1934 the lease was taken over by Imperial College and in 1949 the school moved to Princes Gate and later to Hampton Court. The building was demolished in 1962.

In 1864 the Metropolitan Railway was allowed to extend its 'Inner Circle' line from Paddington to South Kensington, news received with mixed feelings by the builders of the new houses when some villas had to be demolished. In 1907 the construction of the Piccadilly Line necessitated the building of the entrance on the Pelham Road side of the station as seen here. The original plan of Leslie Green, the famous architect of stations, to crown it with a handsome four-storey block of flats, never materialized.

Harrington Road, c. 1900. Note the young violinist crossing the street, on her way perhaps to the Royal College of Music. On her left is the still-existent Norfolk Hotel. The Stanhopes, Earls of Harrington, have owned considerable property in Kensington since the sixteenth century.

The magnificent interior of No. 39 Harrington Gardens as it appeared in 1906 (above). The house was built specially for William Schwenk Gilbert (left) in 1883 when he was celebrating the great financial success of *HMS Pinafore*. The frontage decoration of a ship did not commemorate this, but Gilbert's seafaring ancestor, Sir Humphrey Gilbert. Apart from its grand exterior and lavish internal decorations, the house had electric light, powered by a gas-engined dynamo, and a telephone with a direct line to the Savoy Theatre. The doors to the various rooms bore mottoes, such as 'Abandon hope all ye who enter here' on the dining room!

Debnam Motors *c.* 1920, soon after its opening at 8–15 Athelstone Mews. The property was leased by Henry George Debnam on 21 February 1917, and he converted the existing stables into a garage named initially Golly's Garage. Athelstone Mews, like so many others in the area, was built in the 1870s as stabling with small flats above to serve the big houses, in this case in Cromwell Road. By 1925 Henry was trading under his own name; he held the Daimler franchise in west London. Since the early days Debnam had dealings with royalty, and on his advertising he describes himself as 'an expert to the Royal Families of Great Britain and Europe'. Judging from a series of photographs given to the Kensington Local Studies Department, employees were also involved in the early days of motor racing, often with some success. The firm remained in business until 1972.

EARLS COURT

The Edwardian shopping terrace at the northern end of Earls Court Road c. 1904, when
the homely shops of butchers, drapers and newsagents preceded today's offices and
restaurants. For centuries this had been no more than a leafy lane leading from the high
road towards Chelsea. Those who used it might be on their way to the old manor house, or
Earls Court Farm. By the early nineteenth century, a few cottages, an inn and later a
brewery were clustered around what is known today as 'Earls Court Village', near Kenway
Road. By then Earls Court House, which had been the home of the celebrated surgeon,
John Hunter, had become a lunatic asylum. The Gunter family of prosperous confectioners,
living at Earls Court Lodge (nicknamed Currant Jelly Hall), were beginning to move into
property development and within a century Earls Court was to become a crowded, built-up
urban area and the venue for one of London's most fantastic exhibitions.

Earls Court farmhouse with the Manor House behind, as they appeared in 1874. The hoarding marks the railway crossing under the road at the time of the construction of Earls Court station, which was situated on the east side of the road. The wooden construction burned down in 1875 and was replaced by a more permanent structure on the west side.

The house beyond, known as the Manor House, in 1845. Erected in the 1790s, according to the historian Thomas Faulkner, it replaced an earlier building demolished at that time. It was occupied by the Hutchins family who had been tenants of the estate for many decades. The manor courts were held there, the last recorded being in 1856.

Earls Court Farm in the 1870s. After Samuel Hutchins's death in 1844, most of the land on the western side of the lane was let to a market gardener, Samuel Alloway, who is seen here (above centre, in a bowler hat) with some of his workers, including Mr Goddard and Mr Ives. The Manor House, seen in the background, had been let to several tenants, including one who kept a menagerie there, but both buildings eventually succumbed to the development which followed the coming of the railway.

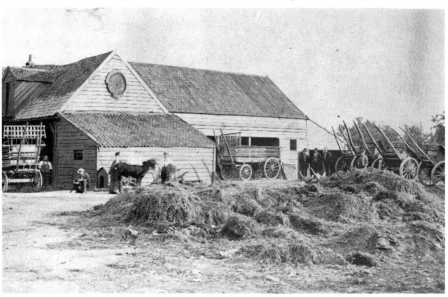

Earls Court House in 1875 about ten years before it was demolished to make way for Barkston Gardens. Situated almost opposite the site of the present station it is, of course, best known for its occupation by the surgeon and anatomist John Hunter, from 1765 to 1793. Hunter's home was the successor to an equally splendid, if not more handsome, house created in the mid-seventeenth century for the Secretary of the Treasury, Henry Guy.

John Hunter (1728–93) kept a menagerie there to further his study of body structure and for medical experiments. A subterranean passage led from the north side of the house to a cloister where the animals were housed, including a den said to have been occupied by a lion and pens for buffaloes, zebras, jackasses and rare breeds of sheep and goats. It was here that he kept the cauldron in which he boiled down the body of the Irish giant to retrieve the skeleton which is still displayed at the Royal College of Surgeons. The feet of the giant can be seen on the right of this engraving of 1814, which was based on Sir Joshua Reynold's portrait.

The southern end of Earls Court Road, near the junction of Barkston Gardens, in early Edwardian days. Parrs Bank, on the corner, was later merged with the Westminster Bank, which still exists as the 'Nat West' in the same terrace.

Late Victorian splendour in the drawing-room of a house in Earls Court Square, *c.* 1880. One of the grandest of the Earls Court developments, started in the 1870s, its residents included Sir William Palliser, landowner, who also made his name as an inventor.

Edwards Furnishing Warehouse at 146 Earls Court Road, photographed from the corner of Trebovir Road in May 1904. The delivery van horse enjoys his nose-bag, and the window display features 'Folding bed, spring overlay mattress and pillow for 17s 9d' and inlaid linoleum for 1s 11d a square yard.

The Old Manor confectionery stores, 175 Earls Court Road, in 1904, 'Proprietors E. Smith & Sons'. The window tells a sweet story: raspberry and vanilla ice creams at 2*d*, 4*d* and 6*d* a glass, Cadbury's chocolate, iced lemonade at 1*d*, 2*d* and 3*d* a glass, and 'Cough No More Lozenges'.

In 1896 a Ladies Cycling Club flourished in the grounds of Hereford Lodge near the corner of Old Brompton Road and Redcliffe Gardens, as shown above. The track was described as 'a miniature Olympian', forming a circle round the grounds and running over two artistic bridges. Hereford Lodge, and its neighbour Coleherne House, on the estate of which the confectioner James Gunter was ground landlord, had already been advertised as building land in 1863 but survived for another thirty years, Coleherne being occupied by Edmund Tattersall, head of the bloodstock auctioneers. Both houses were demolished in 1899–1900 for the building of Coleherne Court, seen below *c.* 1907.

Clareville Cottage, Old Brompton Road, portrayed here by T. Hosmer Shepherd in 1852. The 'Cottage' was described as a new house in 1784 when it and four other villas were built on the land of the Day estate between Gloucester Road and Love Lane (Dove Mews) in 1784. It was demolished in the 1880s.

Clareville Cottage (above) was the residence of the coloratura soprano Jenny Lind on her arrival in London in 1847, when she delighted audiences who dubbed her 'the Swedish Nightingale'. Madame Jenny (Johanna) Lind Goldschmidt (1820–87; right) spent the last part of her life in England, living at 1 Moreton Gardens (189 Old Brompton Road) from 1875 to her death in 1887, when she was singing professor at the Royal College of Music.

These handsome young cowboys gave London another taste of the Wild West in 1909 at the Golden West Exhibition, which attempted to repeat the success of 1887 when the Earls Court Exhibition opened with Colonel William Cody's 'Buffalo Bill's Roughriders and Red Skins Show'. The entrepreneur John Robinson Whitley acquired the six acres of surplus railway land between Warwick Road and Richmond (now Old Brompton) Road in 1884, the rest of the triangular site being occupied by coal depots and railway works. Whitley had seen the wild west show in Washington and booked it as his opening event. At the beginning of 1887 two gangs, each of 1,000 men, worked 24 hours a day in two shifts, for four months, to construct an open arena with a covered stand as well as an exhibition building and pleasure gardens, with a switchback, huge bandstand and other attractions. During its five month season 15,000 visitors came daily to see the show, including the Queen (who was shown a shortened version and asked to meet an Indian papoose), the Prince of Wales, Gladstone and the whole of Harrow School! Whitley followed his first triumph with further exhibitions on national themes, but he never achieved equal success, and by 1891 he had retired. Within three years he had been succeeded by a new entrepreneur, the Hungarian Imre Kiralfy, who had already made a name as the presenter of circuses and spectaculars.

The Big Wheel towering above the Earls Court roof tops, *c.* 1903. It was Imre Kiralfy who added a new sophistication to the Exhibition pleasure gardens with the great wheel and the water shute (see below). The wheel, modelled on the great ferris wheel at Chicago, was constructed in 1894 by an independent company. It was 300 feet in diameter, weighed 1,000 tons and took 20 minutes to complete a revolution (with a pause to allow the passengers to enjoy the view). Its 40 cars, each with 40 passengers, allowed a maximum capacity of 1,600 people. It operated for many years without a serious accident, although a year after it opened in 1895 it stuck for four and a half hours: the passengers were given £5 each for their ordeal.

The water shute, *c.* 1903, was somewhat less spectacular, and like the switchback was said to lose some of its effect because the surrounding rocks and crags were not high enough to block out the view of surrounding chimney pots!

The Exhibition was transformed in Edwardian days to portray the Ice Caverns of Hungary in 1908 (above) and the minarets of a Balkan village in 1907 (below).

Kiralfy had switched his attention to the White City in 1906, but Earls Court continued under new management and presented a series of exhibitions similar to those he had staged with national themes. Many new buildings had been added, such as the huge Empress Theatre (the Empress Hall) – technically in Fulham, as were all the western pleasure gardens – and the Queen's Court with its lake and palace, adaptable to various themes.

Although the grounds remained open until the outbreak of the First World War, the Earls Court Exhibition slowly declined. During the war, the Empress Hall was used to house Belgian refugees, described as 'the largest clearing house in Europe for dealing with the refugee problem'. A chapel was set up for the spiritual comfort of these thousands of families displaced from the battlefields of Flanders. Here the Auxiliary Bishop of Malines, Monsignor De Waechter, is seen blessing the angelus bell presented to the camp chapel by Sir Horace Monro, on 5 February 1915. In the 1920s and '30s much of the area became derelict, apart from some small industries, although the Empress Stadium survived as an ice rink and the site of various entertainments. In 1936 a £1.5 million development roofed over the area to build the modern exhibition buildings, which in recent years have been greatly extended.

Ellen Terry (left, in 1888) moved into 33 Longridge Road in 1878, with her two children Edith and Gordon Craig and her two dogs Drummie and Fussie, soon after her marriage to Charles Wardell. It was here that Sir Henry Irving invited her to join his company at the Lyceum, thus forming one of the most famous partnerships in theatrical history. The Revd Dugald McColl, minister of the Kensington Presbyterian church (later St John's), who lived at No. 36, wrote in his memoirs of the contrast between the dullness of the street with its houses of 'sad coloured brick and window-surrounds in gritty stucco' and its inhabitants. He recalled Ellen Terry's departure for rehearsals thus: 'She appeared on the steps like an April morning . . . the air became tender and gay with wavings and blown kisses; the wheels revolved, and greyness descended once more on Longridge Road.'

Longridge Road in 1905.

Section Nine

BROMPTON AND KNIGHTSBRIDGE

Brompton Road in 1904, crowded with the traffic and shoppers of the time. A century earlier this
was a comparatively quiet country road, only enlivened by the frequency of its inns and a few
scattered cottages. In fact the name 'Brompton Road' was not applied to the old turnpike connecting
Knightsbridge with Fulham until the 1860s, and Cromwell Road was non-existent. Lacking a
bridge over the creek or railway at its western end, it petered out after Earls Court. Building
development did not begin on any scale until the 1780s, when the young architect, Henry
Holland, began to build on Lord Cadogan's estate in the north-east of Chelsea. The turnpike was
still narrow and badly surfaced, but the route to London lay through Knightsbridge and Hyde Park
Corner. In the 1820s further development began with the building of Brompton Square. In 1853
Charles Henry Harrod acquired a small grocery shop in one of the terraces, known as 8 Middle
Queens Buildings, selling humble goods such as tea, soap and candles.

In the 1880s the magnificent Oratory of St Philip Neri began to rise among the towers and domes of the museums area, seen above in 1882. The Oratorians, founded in Rome in 1578, were introduced to England in 1847 by John Henry Newman. They came to Brompton in 1852, where they built an oratory house with a private chapel which was later extended to provide a public church. As this became too small for increasing congregations, funds were raised by public appeal to build a 'cathedral' church. The commission was given to Herbert Gribble. Sadly, Gribble died at the age of forty-seven, and although the oratory was consecrated in April 1884 it was still incomplete. The dome, seen in this 1890s' picture (left), was the design of another architect, George Sherrin.

The Bell and Horns, on the corner of Old Brompton Road and Thurloe Place, in 1914, only a year before its demolition for the development of Empire House. Adjoining the nursery garden of John Harrison, the old coaching inn is recorded as early as 1722 as The Bell. The addition of 'Horns' may have originated with a merger with another inn of that name. The early building was reconstructed in 1824 and enlarged and altered in Victorian times. Work on Empire House, seen to the left and back of the Bell and Horns, was begun in 1910 for the Continental Tyre Company. It was not completed until 1916 due to the continuing presence of the public house.

Brompton Road station in 1908, two years after its opening to serve the new Great Northern, Piccadilly and Brompton Railway (the Piccadilly Line). Brompton Road was closed in the 1930s but the façade remained while the 'ghost station' below was used for defence purposes.

Brompton Square in an engraving, *c.* 1843. This was one of the earliest developments in the area, completed by 1826. The gap at the northern end was the subject of much controversy in the 1840s when the residents of Ennismore Gardens opposed the opening of a road 'to establish links with the aroma of the Serpentine'.

Joyce & Matthews, butchers, seen in 1903 proudly displaying their wares and delivery tricycle. In 1825 a row of five houses was built on the south side of the Brompton Road, now Nos 179–87. The ground floors were converted into shops and in 1888 John Joyce took over the butcher's shop, house and stabling at 183 Brompton Road. Ernest Matthews joined the firm in 1897 and they remained in business until 1927, when the shop was rebuilt as a gallery. The other four properties still survive today.

The original buildings of Harrods Stores, Brompton Road, prior to demolition in 1901. When Charles Henry Harrod opened his first shop in Middle Queens Buildings in what was to become Brompton Road, in 1853, it was hardly a salubrious situation. North Street to the rear was described as 'a mass of filth from one end to the other' and Queens Gardens (later to be swallowed up by the new store) had a rat-infested woodyard. Nevertheless the business prospered, and when he retired for his son Charles Digby Harrod to take over in 1861 it was expanding rapidly, with an extension built over the back garden and a new shop front with a plate glass window proclaiming 'Harrods Stores'. More shops were acquired and, despite a disastrous fire just before Christmas 1883, the business went from success to success. Nevertheless, Mr Harrod never pandered to his customers: he gave them free delivery but was strict about credit and in early days gave none. In 1894 the great decision was taken to rebuild. The design commission went to C.W. Stephens, a hitherto comparatively unknown architect, and the plan was to complete one block 200 × 120 feet every year until the whole store was rebuilt. The interior of the store was, of course, lavish, from its Doulton-tiled meat hall, mahogany, walnut and satinwood counters and furniture, to the ornate ceilings and cornices. The meat hall was built on the site of a small board school which Harrods had great difficulty in acquiring.

Harrods during reconstruction, *c.* 1901–5. At first the intention was to provide a two-storey shop with flats above – partly due to the current fire regulations on the height of shop premises. These flats were huge, sometimes having fifteen rooms, but they were short-lived, and by 1927 the whole building was commercial. So frequent were the alterations that in 1913 a house architect was appointed, and at one time there was a plan to reconstruct along Hans Crescent (below), but this did not materialize. Interestingly it was not until 1921 that the freehold of the site was acquired from its original owners, the Goddard family and their trustees.

The north side of Brompton Road, between Brompton Square and Montpelier Place, *c.* 1900. It has changed much less than other sections, in parts still retaining the old stepped pavements which raised pedestrians above the mud thrown up by the traffic. The big changes here were much earlier, with a row of over fifty terraced houses known as Biscoe's Buildings, then Brompton Row, built in the 1760s.

Rutland Gate in 1905, dated by the hoarding advertising Julia Neilson and Fred Terry in *The Scarlet Pimpernel* at the Vaudeville Theatre. This was a terrace, built in the 1840s opposite Knightsbridge Barracks (described then as 'a range of dull heavy brick buildings badly placed and long an eyesore to the neighbourhood').

Beauchamp Place in 1906, when its humble beginnings were still evident, in contrast to sixty years later when it was described as being 'the steady pulse beat of London fashion'. It was first developed in the early nineteenth century in the midst of financial uncertainty, owing to the many problems of its owner, the sporting gunsmith Joseph Manton. By 1871 half the houses were in multi-occupation and a complaint was made to the Vestry that two were being kept as common brothels!

Knightsbridge (looking east) in 1900 before modern development removed the terrace of houses on the left. The equestrian statue is of Field Marshal Lord Strathnairn, a hero of the Indian Mutiny. It was removed in 1933 when extensive road widening took place.

'Scotch Corner', photographed on 11 September 1902 by Ernest Milner. Officially known as Park Mansions, the imposing block of flats built between 1900 and 1902 in place of a ragged collection of old houses and shops is now best known as 'The Scotch House' from the shop which occupies its groundfloor on the apex of Brompton and Kensington Roads. In 1900 the business was run by Gardiner & Co. Park Mansions Arcade runs beneath the flats to connect the two roads, complementing Brompton Arcade opposite and Knightsbridge Station Arcade (now demolished).

CHELSEA

The last days of the old waterfront at Chelsea, captured by the famous photographer James Hedderley in 1870 from a vantage point in the tower of Chelsea Old Church. Looking west, the trees of Cremorne's pleasure gardens can be seen in the distance. Old Battersea Bridge (left), the frail wooden structure built by Henry Holland a century earlier, was also nearing its demise. Although the proposition to embank the northern shore of the Thames between Vauxhall and Battersea Bridges was first made by the Commissioners of Woods and Forests in 1839, nothing happened for many years owing to the cost of building a new suspension bridge at Chelsea. This did materialize in 1853 but the embankment then petered out at the end of the grounds of the Royal Hospital. The Chelsea Embankment remained a contentious parliamentary issue for nearly twenty years when the plan was drawn up by the great engineer Sir Joseph Bazalgatte.

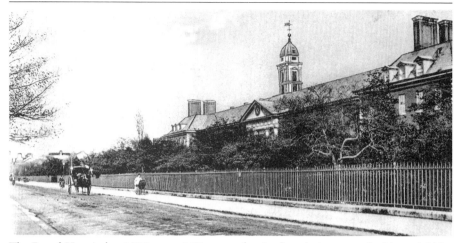

The Royal Hospital *c.* 1900, over 200 years after its foundation stone had been laid by Charles II in 1682. The King's concern for his wounded soldiers had been expressed long ago on the battlefield at Tangiers when he promised them that they would always be in his care. The site chosen was that of the old Chelsea College, a theological institution now defunct and owned by the Royal Society. The land was bought for the Crown for £1300 and Sir Christopher Wren was commissioned to design the building, which was completed in 1692. Apart from some later additions by Robert Adam and Sir John Soane it changed very little until the world wars, when the old soldiers once again came under fire: various parts of the hospital and its grounds were hit, but despite these tragic events most of the original features remain.

Pensioners at the hospital are selected from a huge number of eligible applicants, who must all be on permanent pensions, have no dependents and have given 'good service by flood and field'. The traditional uniform, shown here in 1900, remains, scarlet coat in summer, navy blue in winter, the old fashioned army cap or the ceremonial tricorn. The military structure of administration is also virtually unchanged since its foundation. Although it was thought at first that army discipline might be unwelcome in old age, it is enjoyed by men who have spent long years in service.

Pensioners enjoying the recreation room before the First World War.

The hospital buildings, seen here *c.* 1900, are surrounded by acres of lovely grounds, which every spring house the Chelsea Flower Show of the Royal Horticultural Society, now as much a hallmark of traditional Chelsea as the pensioners themselves. The obelisk, which is now a centre point in the marquee at the Chelsea Flower Show, was erected in 1843 in memory of the officers and men of the 24th Regiment who were killed at Chillianwalla in the Sikh War in 1849.

An early photograph by James Hedderley of Chelsea Physic Garden. A young man rests beside the statue of Sir Hans Sloane, commissioned by the Apothecaries Society in 1757 and executed by Rysbrack. The four acre plot of the Physic Garden was leased to the Society of Apothecaries in 1673 by Sir Charles Cheyne as a Botanical and Physic Garden, but it was not until it came under the patronage of Sir Hans Sloane that its purpose really began to be fulfilled. Sloane studied there as a young man and made his name as a successful and fashionable physician. He had bought the Chelsea Manor estate from the Cheyne family in 1712, and in 1722 gave the freehold of the garden to the Apothecaries Society. Philip Miller was appointed director, an appointment he was to hold for nearly fifty years. Today it thrives as a world-famous centre for the cultivation and study of plants in the expanding science of their use in the treatment of disease, yet the garden still retains its ancient peaceful charm, a gem in Chelsea's crown.

Tite Street in the late nineteenth century, very early in its life. It is named for the Embankment architect Sir William Tite. Its occupants at various times make it one of the best-known thoroughfares, as they include James McNeil Whistler, Oscar Wilde, John Singer Sargent and Augustus John. Whistler's house, White House, designed by Edward Godwin with pale bricks and green slates, aroused great controversy. He only lived in it a short time owing to his bankruptcy following the famous libel action with John Ruskin.

James McNeil Whistler (1834–1903) portrayed in this etching by Paul Cesar Hellen. Whistler may be only one of the stars in Chelsea's galaxy of famous artists, but his life story competes with any of them, with his Irish-American descent and his cosmopolitan education until his settling in Chelsea. His flamboyant life style, behaviour and dress, his conceit, stinging wit and sarcasm have been chronicled as variedly and as often as his artistic genius, which is undeniable.

Cremorne Gardens at the height of its popularity in the mid-1860s. Cremorne House was built in 1740 for the Duke of Huntingdon, whose widow founded the Huntingdon Connexion, a splinter group of Wesleyan Methodists. It was sold in 1785 to Viscount Cremorne who gave it its name. Its later owner, Charles de Berenger Baron de Beaufain, an entrepreneur despite his aristocratic title, opened a sporting club there for 'gentlemen to take manly exercise', and this in turn changed again in 1845, under the promotion of Thomas Bartlett Simpson, to a pleasure garden which became the delight of the masses and the bane of the more select residents of Chelsea. Among its devotees was Whistler, who visited it frequently with Walter and Henry Greaves to enjoy its vivid life and colour, which they frequently portrayed. The entertainment included bands, performances by clowns, giants and dwarfs, performing animals, every conceivable form of side-show, spectacle and sensation and, in the evenings, fireworks – which particularly attracted Whistler and the Greaves. This study by Walter Greaves, a disciple of Whistler, shows that he was an artist of repute in his own right. It includes the figures of Whistler (standing right) and Greaves and his sister sharing a bottle of beer.

CREMORNE

ANOTHER STARTLING NOVELTY
MONDAY, Aug. 7th, 1865,
WHEN THAT EXTRAORDINARY INVENTION
THE AERIAL VESSEL
SAILING BALLOON!
"L'ESPERANCE"

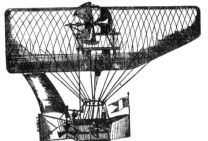

INVENTED AND CONSTRUCTED by M. DELAMARNE.
Will ascend from these Gardens. This novel and remarkable Balloon is the first of the kind ever invented. It is nearly 300 feet in length, 50 feet in diameter, and 150 feet in circumference. Being provided with Screw Propellors and a Rudder, similar to those of a ship, which are set in motion by machinery.
It ascends and descends at will, becoming lighter or heavier than the air, and already much progress has been made towards propelling it in any given direction.
The First Public Experiments made with this Monster Machine were from the Gardens of the Luxemburg in Paris, before the Senate of France and a vast multitude of people, and were crowned with triumphant success.

☞ Remember! on **MONDAY**, August 7th, at **CREMORNE**.
ARLISS & Co., Printers, 15, Great Queen Street.—W.C.

Ballooning was among the biggest attractions at Cremorne Gardens, as seen in this 1865 poster. A balloonist named De Groot, known as 'the Flying Man', attempted in 1874 to descend from a balloon, The Czar, from a height of 5,000 feet by the use of bats' wings thirty-seven feet wide. As the balloon drifted 300 feet above St Luke's Church, De Groot attempted an emergency landing but crashed to his death. In the afternoons Cremorne was a family outing, but after dark drink and rowdiness gave it a bad name and in 1877 its application for a renewal of its licence was refused; the estate was sold for building and the handsome trees sold off as growing timber.

The closing of Cremorne Gardens allowed the Ashburnham Park Nursery, which belonged to the Chelsea gardener and horticulturist James Wimsett, to expand. Although not as famous as his neighbours, such as Veitch, Wimsett was described as a 'distinguished cultivator of rare and valuable plants'. The nursery, seen here in 1903, was sold as a school site in 1907.

Duke Street in 1865, only a few years before it and other old streets and alleyways by the river, such as Lawrence and Lombard Streets, were swept away by the building of the Embankment. This whole area around the Old Church and the approach to Battersea Bridge was the essence of Thames-side Chelsea, with its wharves, docks and boatyards and old taverns such as the Adam and Eve. Mrs Carlyle would have shopped here, in Lombard Street perhaps, where the Elizabethan Arch House spanned the narrow road and where the 'sea tar breeze', described by Thomas Carlyle, was also spiced with the scent of the coal unloading from barges at Alldin's or Johnson's Wharf. Part of this area was used in 1910 for the reconstruction of Crosby Hall, moved from the City stone by stone. One of the objects of the embankment project was to provide a route for the newly improved sewer by reclaiming land from the river, and between Old Church Street and Oakley Street the shore line was moved outwards so that the old trees on the bank now grew in the garden space dividing the buildings from the river.

The south side of Duke Street was the first to go, in 1873, as the great embankment wall went up, putting an end to the tidal floods which could lap the front gardens and the shop doorsteps in Cheyne Walk. The north side of these by-ways also eventually succumbed to more modern buildings, and the sixteenth-century Magpie and Stump, near Oakley Street, burned down in 1886. These two photographs are part of the visual historical record made by James Hedderley of old Chelsea between 1860 and 1875. He worked as a sign writer in the riverside village and at Worlds End. His photographs were taken with a cumbersome 10 × 12 foot plate camera mounted on a tripod.

Chelsea Old Church in its 1870s setting, still the centre of the waterside village as it had been for nearly 800 years. There is a record of a church here in Norman times, but this could have been preceded by a Saxon church. In 1290 it was named as 'Chelchurche of All Saints' in papal letters from Pope Nicholas IV. As the population of Chelsea increased the little church began to be outgrown by its congregation, with noble families complaining that they could not find room in the pews, and in 1670 it was practically rebuilt with a new roof and tower and peal of bells. It was almost totally destroyed by a land mine on 16 April 1941, although the chapel where Thomas More, 'The King's good servant – but God's first –', had sung Offices as humbly as any parish clerk, happily survived. After the bombing the building was boarded up, with the exception of the More Chapel which was repaired sufficiently to enable worship to be continued. The church was rebuilt in 1958 on the old plan to the design of Walter Godfrey, including the restoration of the More Chapel and the repair and replacement of almost all the monuments.

An early twentieth-century photograph of the southern end of Old Church Street. Until the King's private road was opened up, Church Lane (as it was once known) was the only coach way to the riverside village. In later times it was the site of the seventeenth-century Black Lion with its tea gardens and bowling green. Carlyle bought his cigars from a tobacconist's shop here. Among its many famous residents over the years was Dr Francis Atterbury, politician and theologian, and Dr John Arbuthnot, physician to the Royal Hospital. Jonathan Swift lodged there in April 1711, complaining at having to pay six shillings a week for a silly room with coarse sheets!

The Rectory in its heyday at the turn of the century before it became the focus of development wrangles. The seventeenth-century house, with its two acres of garden on the eastern corner of Old Church Street, is one of the largest private estates in London. In 1824 St Luke's in Sydney Street was consecrated as the new parish church, but the first vicar, the Hon. Revd Gerald Wellesley, brother of the Duke of Wellington, continued to live in the Rectory. It was here that Charles Kingsley, author of *The Water Babies*, was brought up when his father was rector in the 1830s.

The seventeenth-century Lindsey House *c.* 1900, now altered and rebuilt to become a terrace of seven houses, 95–100 Cheyne Walk. It was bought in 1750 by Count Zinzendorff, a religious philanthropist, who had befriended the Moravian Brethren, a displaced Protestant sect suffering persecution in Central Europe. Here they led a simple communal life, until their benefactor's death when they were forced to leave, only retaining their chapel and burial ground, which still survive. Among later famous residents were the engineers Marc Isambard and his son Isambard Kingdom Brunel, James Whistler and the boatmen artists Walter and Henry Greaves.

Walter Greaves and Thomas Carlyle, two of Chelsea's most famous residents, in life and effigy in 1890. Note that Greaves still aped the appearance of his master, even though he was rejected by Whistler in later years.

In this photograph of Cheyne Walk in the 1860s (above) the trees that now stand in the embankment gardens were on the river bank (compare the 1905 view, below). The first houses were built on the site of the gardens of Henry VIII's riverside palace, which became the home of the Cheyne family until 1712 when the estate was bought by Sir Hans Sloane, who sold some of the land as building plots. One of the largest and most magnificent was No. 16, which was rented by Dante Gabriel Rossetti in 1862 for £110 a year, where he entertained and worked with all the artists and literati of his time, and kept a menagerie of animals in his back garden.

The Thames Coffee Shop in 1865, run at this time by William Hall. It was situated at the corner of Lawrence Street at No. 51 Cheyne Walk. In the 1860s the row contained five small shops and an inn, the Cricketers, seen to the right of the dining room. All were swept away with the building of the Embankment, and in 1886 Carlyle Mansions occupied the site. The flats were described as having spacious sunny rooms overlooking the river in the front, and less spacious, sunless rooms in the back where the servants slept. Henry James took 21 Carlyle Mansions as his London home in 1913, three years before his death, and wrote to a friend 'this Chelsea perch proves just the thing for me'. The west side of Lawrence Street is believed to be the site of the Chelsea China factory, which thrived from 1745 to 1784 when the works were moved to Derby. Monmouth House, consisting of four houses, was situated at the top of Lawrence Street, and in the 1750s Tobias Smollett, the novelist, and Sir John Fielding, the Bow Street magistrate, were neighbours of the Duchess of Monmouth.

Cheyne Walk looking west from the King's Head and Eight Bells, *c*. 1871. When he came to live in Cheyne Row in 1834, Thomas Carlyle described Cheyne Walk as 'having really good old brick mansions, flagged pavement and a wide carriageway between two rows of stubbornly high old trees'. He was able to enjoy the company of his friend, Leigh Hunt, in Upper Cheyne Row and they were certainly well provided with nearby inns, from the King's Head and Eight Bells on the corner of his street ('Pale Ale 4*d* a pint, Guinness and Bitter 2*d*') to the Thames Coffee House – far from teetotal – at Lawrence Street. Although Mrs Carlyle preferred to have her ham and butter sent from their family in Scotland, she did patronize local shops, Carless the butcher, the Lombard Street fishmonger and local milkmen and bakers. When these photographs were taken by Hedderley, poor Jane Carlyle was sadly no more, having died suddenly while out driving in April 1866, and Thomas was a lonely eccentric old man, wandering about the Chelsea streets like a ghost in his long coat and wide-brimmed hat.

Dr Phene's fantastical house on the corner of Oakley Street in its brief Edwardian days. Of Chelsea's wealth of eccentrics, Dr John Samuel Phene is among the most celebrated, and the 'Chateau' he built is the most extraordinary of its buildings. The highly ornamented edifice, smothered with serpentine bodies, gargoyles, beasts, birds, gods and goddesses, dragons and serpents, picked out in scarlet and gold, gave rise to myths and rumours from its construction in 1906 to its demolition in 1917. Even before the house was built the gardens had been filled with similar creations.

A scholar and antiquarian, Dr Phene (1823–1912) was a knowledgeable eccentric, a pioneer of the now accepted theory that trees purify the air in towns, and was able to convince Victorian developers to plant them whenever possible. He designed many conventional houses in Oakley Street (where he lived himself, never occupying his chateau) and Margaretta Terrace, said to be named for the woman he loved who is rumoured to have died shortly after their marriage.

Oakley Street in the early twentieth century, only a few years after the days when Oscar Wilde had been lionized by his mother's guests, and where he stayed in the agonizing intervals between his trials. The building of the Albert suspension bridge in 1873 made Oakley Street into a main road, although its proximity to Chelsea's Steamboat Company's Cadogan Pier and the Pier Hotel had already made it of some importance to travellers.

Argyll House in the 1900s. It still exists on the corner of Oakley Street and Kings Road, and owes its name from a fairly brief residence by the Duke of Argyll, although it was built in 1723 for John Perrin, whose monogram appears on the gate. It was designed by the famous Venetian architect Giacomo Leoni, and described by him as having 'a beautiful harmony of colours in its brick work and stone decoration'.

Chelsea. Six Bells and Town Hall.

Kings Road in 1900, when the eighteenth-century Six Bells public house had just been rebuilt. Once a medieval cart track used only by farmers and gardeners, Kings Road attained its royal status when Charles II used it as his private road to Hampton Court. It eventually opened to the public in the 1830s.

The Chelsea Palace music hall, seen here *c*. 1900, replaced the Wilkinson Sword factory in 1902 and attracted all the leading stars of the day. After its use as a TV studio from 1956, it was eventually demolished in 1966 and replaced by shops and offices.

Augustus John presiding at the opening of the Chenil Galleries in 1905. Founded by Charles Chenil to help young artists show their work, it stood on the site of the famous Chelsea Arts Club, a meeting place for artists founded in 1891 by the sculptor Thomas Stirling, together with others such as Walter Sickert and Whistler. Augustus John could compete with any of his predecessors or contemporaries in the sensational Chelsea scene as he held court in Kings Road, the Café Royal or anywhere else that artists congregated, in his broad-brimmed hat and flowing cravat. The Arts Club moved to Old Church Street from where it introduced the Chelsea Arts Ball, held first at the nearby Town Hall, then in 1908 at the Royal Opera House Covent Garden, and from 1910 at the Royal Albert Hall. On the opposite side of the road the Board of Guardians building can be seen, later to become Chelsea Registry Office and more recently offices. Next to this is Dovehouse Green burial ground.

Belle Vue Lodge (above, *c.* 1870), on the corner of Beaufort Street, was occupied for a time by Luke Thomas Flood, a benefactor of Chelsea parish. Flood Street (below, *c.* 1905) was named for him, and not for its proximity to the river. Flood Street was once Robinsons Lane and it may well have been down this that Pepys rode to the Swan Inn on the river, famed for its association with the Doggetts Coat and Badge race rowed by the Thames watermen.

Flood Street, Chelsea

In 1888 Lord Cadogan laid the foundation stone of Chelsea's first public library in Manresa Road. A vigorous campaign had been conducted by the supporters of the public library movement, led by Mr B.W. Linden, resulting in the adoption by the Vestry of the Public Libraries Act, and in 1887 two rooms were fitted up as reading rooms in the old Chelsea Vestry Hall. The new library, in Italianate style, was designed by J.M. Bryden, who was also responsible for the Town Hall in 1906. After the amalgamation of the boroughs of Kensington and Chelsea the Manresa Road library was closed and the library moved to the Old Town Hall in 1978.

Sydney Street *c.* 1900, in the days of the early motor buses, bicycles and boaters. Sydney Street commemorates one of the Smith Charity trustees, Viscount Sydney. To the left was St Luke's Infirmary and workhouse and to the right, in the distance, is the ambitious buttressed tower of St Luke's Church, consecrated in 1824. Charles Dickens was married to Catherine Hogarth there in 1836.

Brompton Fire Station soon after its opening in June 1893 on the north side of Trafalgar Square (now Chelsea Square). The new building at South Parade contained one steamer, one manual, one horse cart and one fire escape, with accommodation for eleven men and one coachman. The building, with its 800 foot watchtower, cost £7,862. At the opening the Commissary General remarked that its name was a misnomer as 'it ought to have been Chelsea'. One of the station's most famous inmates in the 1930s was a dog rumoured to stamp out fires with its paws. The station closed when the new Chelsea station was opened on the Kings Road in 1964.

Fulham Road at the junction with Old Church Street in 1900. The original Queen's Elm inn is meant to commemorate the spot where Lord Burghley once walked with Queen Elizabeth I and took shelter from the rain under an elm in the Fulham Road.

Fulham Road in the early 1900s. Stocken and Co. (on the right) proudly announce they are 'Carriage and Motor Builders to the King and the Prince of Wales'. The picture is taken from the corner of Drayton Gardens looking westward. The two cyclists are telegraph boys.

This very early photograph (*c.* 1864) shows the south side of Sloane Square at about the same time that the Welsh draper Peter Rees Jones came to London to seek his fortune (see p. 156). The square was only a part of the ambitious plan of Henry Holland, the eighteenth-century builder/architect who developed Hans Town, the whole area between Kings and Brompton Roads. The son of a Fulham master builder, Holland leased 85 acres of farmlands known as Blacklands from Lord Cadogan in 1771, although building did not begin for another eight or nine years. Holland retained a generous portion for his own house, The Pavilion, and its extensive gardens, most of which later became Cadogan Square, named for the family linked to Hans Sloane by the marriage of his daughter to the second Baron Oakley, Charles Cadogan. Meandering through Blacklands on its way to the Thames, the Westbourne river was crossed in the region of Sloane Square by Bloody or Blandel Bridge, and its waters still flow through a conduit over the District and Inner Circle lines at Sloane Square station. When first laid out, the centre of the square was no more than a grass patch surrounded by a chain fence, later replaced by railings, where Queen Charlotte's Volunteers drilled and boys played cricket.

The south-west corner of Sloane Square nearest to Kings Road, photographed around 1890, shows some humble shops with goods hanging outside, a patent piano maker and an Aerated Bread Company shop, which were rebuilt soon afterwards. After the Kings Road was opened to the public in 1830, shops began to intersperse the villas along the highway until in modern times it became one of the world's most famous thoroughfares. The road reached its zenith in the 'swinging sixties' and the arrival of Mary Quant. In a few short years all the small useful neighbourhood shops closed as the boutique owners moved in. The 'beautiful people' of the sixties were followed in the 1970s by the punks.

This photograph, taken in 1864, shows the west side of Sloane Square before another success story was written. In 1877 Peter Jones took over Nos 4 and 6 Kings Road, near the corner pub, the Star and Garter, previously occupied by a linen draper. Young Mr Jones had come to London ten years earlier, and after a few years as an apprentice he saved enough to acquire two shops in Marlborough Road (Draycott Avenue) to open his own Co-operative Drapery. It was while these were being knocked into one that the building collapsed, killing an apprentice workman and burying his wife in the debris. She survived and the shocked Jones and his few assistants recovered, the shop was rebuilt and within a few more years moved to the Sloane Square premises between a boot warehouse and a grocer. The business went from strength to strength and by 1894 had spread to the twelve next door houses, and was employing a staff of 200. On his death in 1905 it was bought by another Welsh draper, John Lewis, from Oxford Street. In 1935 Peter Jones's red brick, green roofed store was pulled down and replaced by the modern six-storey building which now dominates the west end of the square.

Workmen on the roof of Sloane Square House in 1893. Over the next ten years great changes were to take place on the square, including the south-east corner with the rise of the Royal Court theatre. In 1871 the Ranelagh Chapel, built in 1817, became the Royal Court theatre, a site next to the station which had actually been used as a theatre much earlier. Its first proprietor, Bertie Crewe, was succeeded by Harvey Granville Barker and J.E. Vedrenne in 1904, in whose hands the theatre earned the reputation for progressive productions which it has never lost, despite the ups and downs of nearly a century. Under this management eleven Bernard Shaw plays were presented, six for the first time, as well as Galsworthy's *Silver Box* and Granville Barker's own play *The Voysey Inheritance*. In 1935 the Royal Court became a cinema; it suffered severe bomb damage in 1940. Rebuilt in 1954, it was soon taken over by George Devine and his English Stage Company, whose third production was John Osborne's *Look Back in Anger*, followed by a series of successes with work by young dramatists such as Harold Pinter, Arnold Wesker and Samuel Beckett.

This 1900 view of Sloane Square shows the late Victorian changes, with hotels and mansion blocks replacing domestic shops. In 1953 an ornamental fountain was set up at this end, designed by Gilbert Ledward, as a gift from the Royal Academy to Chelsea. The square continues to change as old buildings change hands or are modernized.

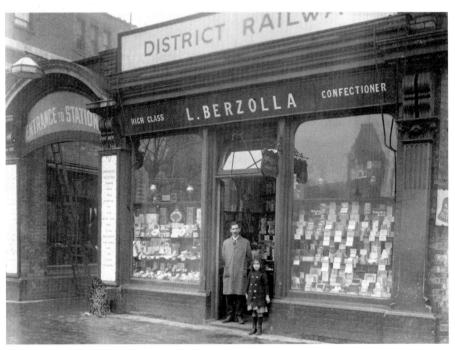

Berzolla's confectionery shop in 1927, next to the entrance to Sloane Square station. The Berzolla family, who ran the business here from 1918 to 1938, donated the photograph to Chelsea Library.

The north end of Sloane Street, *c.* 1900. In 1830 the Church of Holy Trinity was built to the design of James Savage, a Gothic revival building which lasted sixty years, being replaced in 1890 by the present church by J.D. Sedding. It has been described as a cathedral of arts and crafts, and includes decoration by William Morris and Burne-Jones. Beloved by John Betjeman, it was saved from extinction some years ago. Betjeman also immortalized the Cadogan Hotel, Sloane Street, in his poem about Wilde's arrest there in 1895.

Nathalie's at 187A Sloane Street after 1891, when she moved from No. 189. Mme Leah Nathalie, seen here at the doorway, opened her fan-making shop in the mid 1880s. She continued in business until 1912, by which time fans were no longer an essential fashion accessory.

Chelsea Creek, the boundary between Chelsea and Fulham caught by the lens of James Hedderley when it was still at the height of its industrial importance at the end of the nineteenth century. This was almost the last of the Chelsea riverside to be swept away by modern development, in the shape of Chelsea Harbour. The creek was the outlet of the stream originally known by several names, such as Billingswell Ditch and Counters Creek, which arose near Kensal Green and pursued a roughly straight course south-east along the border of Kensington and Hammersmith, crossed by bridges on Hammersmith Road, Fulham Road (Stamford) and Kings Road (Stanley). In 1828 an attempt was made to convert the lower two miles into a canal which could take vessels up to 100 tons burden, with timber, coal and sand to a basin near the present site of Olympia. This was not a success, and after less than twenty years the canal was drained to create the Western Extension railway line, pilloried in the 1840s as Mr Punch's Railway, and the stream became a sewer. The inlet was described as recently as 1952 as being 'still visible as a stagnant ditch with a few disheartened marguerite daisies and thistles growing beside the green slime'. The area was chosen for an expensive development when twenty acres of coal yards were bought by P & O and Globe in the 1980s to create Chelsea Harbour, described as a 'unique world of houses, flats, offices, restaurants and shops, achieving a complete transformation'.